The Homeschooling Parent

Self-care and Feeding for the Person Who Makes It All Happen

Kerridwen Mangala McNamara, M.S.

Ivory Tower Lair
An Imprint of Rising Dragon Books

The Homeschooling Parent: Self-care and Feeding of the Person Who Makes It All Happen
Copyright © 2022 by Ivory Tower Lair, an imprint of Rising Dragon Books.
Cover art and illustrations by the author
For further information, email RisingDragonBooks@gmail.com

Book and Cover design by author. Book Formatting inspired by Derek Murphy @Creativindie

ISBN: 978-1-960160-00-3

First Print Edition: December 2022

10 9 8 7 6 5 4 3 2 1

Dedicated to my mom,
without whom I would never have been homeschooled
and therefore this book would never have existed.

Aranyani S. Bhate (1939-2009)
Dancer, folklorist, bibliophile, world-traveler

KERRIDWEN MANGALA MCNAMARA

CONTENTS

Introduction: Homeschooling for Parents

(because the kids are only half the story)

SO YOU'VE DECIDED to homeschool.

Most of us make this jump because of the kid(s). We have a child who is struggling with some aspect of 'traditional' education. We have a baby and can't quite imagine turning that sweet child over to a system that we didn't enjoy ourselves. Or maybe it's out of fear – we're pulling the kids out because of Covid or masks or school shootings or drugs or our political or moral values or religious beliefs. And sometimes it's about the things we hope to offer our kids: *more* opportunities, a *better* fit with curriculum, *choices* for what they are learning (or about the pace or style).

There are also some parents who will admit that they choose to homeschool because they want to take the whole family traveling or for family togetherness in some other facet. But it's still *framed* as being about the kids when they explain their choices to other parents, friends, *their* parents and in-laws, maybe even the kids' *other* parent... maybe even to themselves.

And why?

Kids are super-important, and choosing to homeschool yours is a pretty out-there-in-everyone's-face declaration that you are putting them ahead of everything else.

But.

Parents are important, too, and – to be entirely honest – the Good Ship Homeschool runs aground more often with parents than with kids.

My contention here is that this is because we, as parents, don't do a good job of recognizing our needs in a useful and healthy way. We've all been the mom or dad who struggled on to go to work, get healthy (or at least edible) food on the table, read stories, listen to the teenage angst, and finally get everyone into bed... all while struggling with the flu or pneumonia or some longer-term condition. Some of us even put ourselves into the hospital that way... or simply collapse slowly of 'small' chronic conditions that add up over time.

I've done it myself. I've done it *more than once,* turning into the Overburdened Caregiver, and I still have to remind myself not to do it anymore.

I have to remind myself to avoid that route. *Not* because it's not good for the kids to have that as a role model – though I do want *them* to learn to take better care of themselves. And *not* because I want to have grandchildren someday (some very, very far away day!). And not even because it's hard on my long-suffering spouse.

I have to remind myself not to become the Overburdened Caregiver because this is *my* life and I deserve to enjoy it as much as the kids deserve to enjoy theirs.

So, that said, I'll admit it.

One of the main reasons I homeschool my kids is so that I can sleep in.

SLEEPING IN WAS NOT MY reason at the beginning of our homeschool journey. I had all those grand, wonderful ideas about providing the ideal educational atmosphere. I'd been homeschooled from second through twelfth grade myself (more about that later) and had a supportive husband who was familiar with the concept.

I was going to do it *even better* than my parents.

After all, *I* knew homeschooling from having been a homeschooled kid. And I had at least a wisp of understanding of it from the other side, having been of some assistance with my ten-years-younger sister (or so I thought).

My version was going to be *better* because I was starting at the beginning – not dumping my precious babies into a system that I'd hated in just two short years. (And, yes, that was kindergarten and first grade: the 'fun' years.) I was going to do everything with *intention,* rather than *ad hoc.*

Part of this mindset was also enhanced by falling into the edges of a Waldorf School community, first in Ann Arbor, MI, and then in Louisville, KY. The idea of being *intentional* – of *crafting* a life of beautiful, handmade objects and efforts – was extremely appealing to me. My dear, long-suffering husband went along with things for the most part.

But... he's also always been the one to put a bit of a break on my wild ideas.

Not so much *verbally* as by modeling the more sensible approach... sometimes even when he doesn't notice what he's doing.

It was my dear husband – and he will deny this, I suspect – who made me realize that sleeping in was why I wanted to homeschool.

DEFINITION
Ambisleptic: to sleep both night and day

We were taking part in a wonderful little Saturday morning 'Parent-Child' class at our local Waldorf school. The teacher, Miss Angie, was thrilled to have both parents along – even if it meant we brought our four-year-old, who was really too old for the class, along with our two-year-old and baby. At four, our oldest daughter was eligible to be enrolled in their Kindergarten program, which I was attracted to except for (1) the cost and (2) that I really wanted to homeschool her.

At that point my biggest argument for homeschooling (and it's still important) is that, after doing all the hard work to get my child potty-trained, weaned, and using some manners... why should someone *else* have all the fun of getting to be there at the instant she learned to read or figure out addition? That was supposed to be *my* reward for all those mounds of dirty diapers (mostly cloth... that's where I was in the cycle in those days) and the crying and the late-night nursing.

The local Waldorf School was only a five-minute drive away. We could have *walked* there with a little gumption, though two toddlers and a baby made and no real sidewalks made that idea... undesirable.

Five minutes away... and yet we were *always* five minutes late.

And I was *always* pulling my hair out (metaphorically) in my frustration at trying to get everyone out of the house. I'd be grumpy with husband and children for the first ten or twenty minutes of a 'class' that was all about building a sense of serenity and security into a child's life.

And we did this for *over two years!*

It was while I was pregnant with my fourth child that I finally gave up. I decided we would take a 'break' from the Parent-Child classes, much as we loved them – and where all of us always enjoyed the time... eventually – because I was worn out with getting everyone up on Saturday morning.

Plain and simple: sleeping in was more important to our family than this activity we all enjoyed. Much more recently, the kids and I invented a word for this preference: we're 'ambisleptic'.

I WISH I COULD SAY I never looked back.

But I'm me, and there's always *some* activity that we end up becoming deeply involved in that serves as an engine for the family; something that makes us get up and go. Though I *did* learn to try to avoid activities that happen in the morning. Even on weekdays.

Lego teams, Math Circles, gymnastics meets and chess tournaments... and a variety of other things have captivated my family's interest over the years. When it starts to feel like *captured* is the operative term instead of *captivated,* it's time for our family to back off and seek a better balance. (And by 'our family', I usually mean *me*. It's my job in our family to be the one who figures that stuff out usually – with the help of my husband and kids, but I'm The Scheduler, so I have to have some sense of what is insane instead of intense.)

And mostly I can see the danger signs on the horizon now... or even anticipate when crunch-times will put us at risk. The kids and my husband have learned to keep an eye out as well, and to heed my warning signs as well *because*...

...it's *also* usually me who has the physical or emotional reaction to us trying to *do too much* – from grumpiness and brusqueness to stomach cramping and weeping. They don't like seeing me in that state. And they're willing to forgo the occasional fun thing to keep me healthy.

And it's not because I am MOM and without me the whole shebang collapses.

It's because I'm Mom (and Wife) and they love me – and they want me to enjoy life as much as they do.

Because I *deserve* to enjoy my life – in their words.

So... just who am I, and why should you trust me?

MY PARENTS BEGAN HOMESCHOOLING ME at the beginning of second grade to help me through stress-induced (school-induced) migraine headaches. Both of my parents had loved school (they were those annoying people who always aced the tests and never seemed to study... I most certainly am *not*, but they say you marry someone like your parent...). Homeschooling was the absolute last thing they tried.

And I do mean *the last*.

They had my pediatrician test me for everything from epilepsy to diabetes. She, in turn, decided I was bored in school and that I should be put ahead a grade (this was the ancient of days in the '70s when you weren't supposed to know how to read on entering Kindergarten... and I did). The school... did not appreciate 'interference' from parents or doctors and 'went along with it' only to make the implementation impossible.

After fighting through this morass for two solid years, my mom – in desperation – decided to find out if this crazy idea she'd been reading about was legal in New York State. The Department of Education attorney whom she'd made an appointment with dissed her and left a junior attorney to answer her questions... who just happened to be homeschooling his own kids and had all the details right at his fingertips.

At the time, New York State had no real rules regarding homeschoolers – so long as your kids weren't going become a burden on the State when they grew up, and the government had to prove it would be a problem. Parents were assumed to be doing a good job! NY is one of the *most* complex states to homeschool in nowadays, but in 1980 there were few enough of us that they hadn't yet created rules.

The school district wasn't exactly thrilled with *this* sort of 'interference' either. They made my parents talk to the District Psychologist who actually told my dad to 'go back to India' if he wanted to do such crazy things. (My dad is an engineer from Mumbai, Maharashtra, India. My mom was a folklorist and dancer from Cleveland, Ohio, USA.) This was not just insulting, but baffling, as homeschooling wasn't really a thing in India then (nor is it much of one now). However, by the law, my parents could legally homeschool me, so they did.

Ten years later, the same year I started college, they began homeschooling my sister, at the beginning of third grade, because she was being bullied in this same school. And, by the way, this was a rich, suburban school district that was supposed to be one of The Best in NY at the time.

Ironically, after all of this, my parents were still extremely pro-school. They tried very hard to talk me into going back to school for high school. They insisted we take every standardized test they could lay hands on and that the school would administer.

And they were absolutely baffled that I wanted to homeschool *my* kids.

They were very effective as our teachers, however. My sister went to an Ivy League university, got a dual degree in Electrical Engineering and Dance and now works at a major defense contractor. I went to a then-top-25 engineering university (as a Biology major – gotta be weird!) and then the top grad school in my field.

My father *does* have a PhD, but he wasn't all that involved in our education. He set expectations, and he was 'available ' to answer questions... But even when he started his own engineering consulting business at home, we were supposed to keep quiet and leave him alone during business hours as much as we could.

It was my mother – with her 1950s High School diploma – who worked with us in a curious mixture of school-at-home (the school district exerted what control they could by giving us the schoolbooks we'd have been using in their classes) and unschooling. Her career, as first an international folkdancer specializing in dances from Eastern Europe and India, and then as a storyteller who could eventually – by heart – tell stories from any nation in the United Nations, was all self-taught, self-sought-out knowledge and wisdom. She read widely and was interested in almost everything – but absolutely flat-out refused to have anything to do with chess or computers. She took us to political protests, including the huge one in NY City that led to the SALT II talks, and found us lessons or learning groups in drum, flute, karate, theater, singing, fencing, gymnastics, stamp-collecting, Star Trek, embroidery, and more varieties of dance than I can name, supporting our interests and nudging us into things we'd never have imagined trying.

From my father and mother both I learned that learning is lifelong and entrepreneurial. You can do anything you set your mind to, so long as you don't start out by shooting yourself in the foot and tell yourself you can't, that it's too hard, that you'll fail.

And that on the days you *do* tell yourself all those things – and there *will* be those days – or that you tell those things to every living human in the reach of your voice... that you also listen, somehow, to the people who are willing to tell you it's not so. Because you have to listen to all those people who have seen what an awesome, amazing person you are and are willing to tell you about it when you can't see it for yourself.

And even super-introverts, like me, need to find those people.

I'm the mom of six homeschooled kids, ranging from a twenty-year-old entering her third year of college away from home to a nine-year-old who insists she will live with us forever and ever. Two have graduated – our second child is heading off to college as I write.

Three of my kids are girls, three are boys – most of them are probably on the ADHD/Autism spectrum – enough so you can see some of it and so that we have ended up having to deal with a variety of Issues, but not so much that we've needed formal diagnoses (since they are at home and we can be flexible). We have three teenagers at home right now and all the parenting crazy that goes with that, from existential crises to career crises. (Okay, so we haven't – yet – had gender-identity crises, but we have dear friends sorting that one out, so we're seeing it at close secondhand. And our kids seem to be uninterested in dating until a little later... not sure if that's gymnastics, genetics, homeschooling... or living out in a rural area without a lot of other options in easy reach.)

All of my children are bright, energetic people who drive me crazy and make me unbearably proud by turns – like all kids. They're all over the introvert/extravert spectrum as well, ranging from the one who would stay in his room all day long if we let him (I'm with him on this one... well, different rooms, we're *introverts* after all!) to the one who is an absolute flaming extravert and Needs People A Lot *(a LOT)*.

The kids (and parents) all have passionate, deep interests – some of them (us) hold onto those interests for years (or life) and others switch regularly. Some of them are big and bold about their interests – some are... I won't say *secretive*, but more *private* about what they love. (And that does *not* split neatly down introvert/extravert lines.)

You'll see some anecdotes about my kids throughout the book. One of them is very protective of his privacy (we're currently studying the development of the Right to Privacy as a pet project of his). I have begun joking that I have five kids and one Red Hoodie, since he would prefer not to show his face in family pictures if I might post them on social media. Partly to preserve his privacy and partly to keep things in context, I describe the kids by their ages in the anecdotes. If a particular story is about my now-twenty-year-old, but she was five at the time, I'll call her my 'then five-year-old.' (I do similar things with the stories of other friends – parents and children both – who get mentions, so that it's not all just my experiences you're reading about.)

My husband is a professor at a large state university and while he's supportive of homeschooling, we don't always see eye to eye on how we're doing, what we're doing, and whether we're making adequate progress to get there (and where *there* is). Sometimes our discussions are thoughtful and careful... sometimes they are, um, *passionate*. My husband does like to do things with the kids and will take them out to teach them how to use power tools like chainsaws and drills... or sit them all down and teach them to do math in binary. His involvement in our homeschooling is deep and intrinsic... but not always consistent, nor does it always fit into my own Grandiose Plans. Learning how to leave space for his sudden desire to have everyone do a 'unit study' on baseball or Steve Jobs or whatever comes up next has been a challenge – but one that the whole family has grown stronger for having to do.

(A secret theme of this book may be that *flexibility* is a far more important parenting skill than *consistency*. We all need a balance between these extremes: yours will be at a different place than mine. But keep in mind that this is a moving target. My point for balance started out much heavier on the *consistency* side – I read all those parenting books, too – and in edging back from that precipice we've sometimes overshot on the *flexibility* side. No one died, so it was a growth and learning experience for all of us!)

What this book is about

THIS BOOK IS ABOUT HOW to take care of yourself as a homeschooling parent.

But more than that, it's about how to make sure you get at least as much out of the whole experience as your kids do.

If you need another incentive – your kids will learn more and be happier, your spouse or S.O. will be less stressed, your parents might bug you a little bit less, and you'll probably even save money in the long run.

Curious? Let's get started and I'll show you why and how!

P.S. All the "To-Do" sheets from the ends of each chapter, as well as all the other graphics, are available at my website as PDFs so you can easily print them: (https://www.RisingDragonBooks.com)

Chapter One

Choose Homeschooling for YOU, too

SLEEPING IN ISN'T anyone's real Plan for homeschooling, but it might end up being either (or both) a perk and a coping technique.

When you elect to homeschool your kid(s) you are making a choice that is going to change your life in a big way. You can try to manage this change by fighting it and wrestling it to the ground, but it's going to turn into a tickle-fight and we all know that the kids sometimes win those when they find our ticklish spots.

Or you can take a slightly less top-down approach.

And I will tell you: that less top-down approach can be *scary*, even for someone who came at it as a former homeschooled kid! I watched my public-schooled husband find it even *more* scary. So, believe me, I get it.

Let's be clear. I am *not* suggesting ditching all parenting at any time. The kids need us, and we all signed on to the parenting thing one way or another, so it's our responsibility. Nor am I suggesting letting the kids run everything (not *necessarily*... see Chapter Five on my Family Democracy Journey if you wonder if that could work). And finally, I

1

am *not* suggesting you don't do everything within your abilities to help your kid(s) learn what they can and will absorb.

What I *am* suggesting is that you find a way to embrace homeschooling as a thing you are *choosing*. Not as something that you are being forced into (even if you kind of feel you are). Not as the best of bad choices. Not as an annoying interruption in your career or a financial hit or yet another reason to have to argue with your parents (or in-laws or siblings or friends...)

We know it's all of those things – and I'm no stranger to any of those concerns, trust me. My husband, friends, and kids could tell you how much I moan and groan about those things on occasion.

The critical phrase there, though, is *on occasion*.

When you find yourself resenting – or on the verge of resenting – the kids, the spouse, *or the homeschooling aspect* of life, it's time to take a good hard look at what you're doing.

And yes, I'm including all of you who tell yourself – with increasingly-plastered-on smiles and jaws that are getting a bit sore – that you *do not* resent any of it, you *could never* resent any of it, these are *choices you made...* and so on and so forth. You may be a better human than me, but I'm convinced none of us are really that saintlike parent 100% of the time, or even 100% of the time in front of the kids.

I'm here to tell you *it's okay.*

Your kids will probably not be deeply harmed by having you admit that sometimes you wish you had chosen a different path through life that didn't include them. Will they end up in therapy? Possibly – but don't we all these days? So long as the kids know that you made the best choices that you could and sometimes you spent a little time imagining have taken a different path... the fact that you told them about it once or twice probably won't even be on their top ten list to discuss with their therapist. (There are exceptions to this, as there are to everything. See the box: 'CAVEAT for Dealing with Extremely Sensitive Souls.')

I'm claiming homeschooling should be *about you, too.*

CAVEAT for Dealing with Extremely Sensitive Souls!

There are some particularly sensitive souls – kids and spouses both – and they require special emotional care and feeding. I suspect in some sense it's *even more* important that they hear those things so that they can learn to forgive themselves when *they* feel that way, but finding a way to explain that your emotions are temporary but your love is permanent can be a challenge. If you have – or are – one of these extremely sensitive souls, please make sure you have a solid person outside your family to bounce your frustrations off on, someone who can give you good feedback whether they are a friend, family member, mentor, spiritual advisor, or paid wise person. I've used a variety of these sources – sometimes a paid counselor is what you need and sometimes it's a friend and a box of tissues. There's no shame in any of it and there are free counseling services available to a lot of people, even if it's only one or two sessions.

What does that even mean?

To me it means:

- that I don't dread getting up each morning – if I am hanging out in bed to do some thinking, it's because I decided I wanted to do that and because I *can* do that now that even my youngest kids can feed themselves and largely solve each other's problems. They know where I am and that they can get me up if needed.

  So... SLEEPING IN ISN'T A "GUILTY PLEASURE" for me. It's just a part of life when I need or want it to be.

- that I get to spend *some* amount of time every day and every week doing things *I* want to do. When the kids were younger and needier, that was projects that could be quickly completed or set down and picked up again. Since they've grown, it's back to my writing. The kids actually are happier with me now that I'm doing something that fills my soul – even if I'm actually doing *less* with them.

- that the chores are distributed. I have a lot (A LOT) more to say about chores, but we'll leave that for Chapter Five. Suffice it for now to say that it's good for me when the kids and my husband have responsibilities around the house, but it's also good for *them*.

- that the kids are willing to talk to me (and talk and talk and talk...) about their interests, their dreams, their worries, their concerns. And that I spend enough time with them that I have some sense of when to get up and go do something with them, when to zone them out (those hour-long descriptions of ten-minute Minecraft videos that they watched...), when to try to problem solve *for* them, when to try to problem solve *with* them, when to be excited for them, when to be sympathetic, and when to just be a good ear and a comforting shoulder. I get this wrong as often as anyone, but the kids say I get it right often *enough*.

- that the kids – and my husband – think I'm worth listening to and I can share some of *my* interests, dreams, worries, and concerns (as appropriate). I can see them all – including my husband – zoning out when I'm grumpy, resentful, or whiny. I can see them caring about me when I'm sick, tired, or overwhelmed, but that wears them out. It's much more fun the other way...

...and *that* means *having* something interesting or fun or thoughtful to share with them. That doesn't come from burying myself in worksheets and grading. It *does* come from learning something new, trying something, finishing (or starting) something, exploring *something* (or somewhere), meeting people... In other words, it means doing something that everyone in the family didn't experience with me – that can be through my job, through a club, through a book, a video, a class I'm taking, or any other source.

At this point you may be thinking *"Oh, my goodness! I don't have the time to get everything done as it is, let alone all that, too!"* Or you may be noticing that I haven't added some of the things that are meaningful to you. We'll each have our own lists, of course, but this is like those ads for the closet-organizing companies – we all know that if our closets were organized it would make our lives easier, save us time and effort... but finding the time to *get* organized... in order to get our closets organized isn't easy. Neither is finding the time and energy to re-organize our lives to be a better fit to... our lives.

That's okay, too.

There are times in life when I haven't met more than a couple of these goals for myself. Sometimes it's just nose-to-the-grindstone and you have to get past a chunk of time. In those days we've eaten a lot of fast food, for example, even though we have some health issues that are impacted by that and all of us (except whomever the youngest kid was then – the youngest is always a McDonald's addict, apparently by definition) would prefer a homecooked meal.

This is where I cue up Billy Joel's song *'You're Only Human (Second Wind).'*

(https://www.billyjoel.com/song/youre-only-human-second-wind-2/)

These times *will* come to an end.

Hopefully it's an end you can see – like the End of Diapers or the End of Everyone Having A Stomach Virus All At Once. The ones that are much longer term – like a chronic illness that affects you or someone whom you love and need to care for to some degree – are harder... but since you have more time to cope you also have more opportunities to find coping mechanisms. (As we go on, I'll share some of the ones I've seen people use, and some of the ones I've used myself, for long-term issues.)

But *on an average day* you shouldn't be thinking *"man, my life sucks."* I don't always want to get up in the morning – but that's because I'm more of a night owl and I'm dealing with some long-term fatigue-inducing issues.

So, the question becomes: *what are YOU, the Homeschooling Parent, getting out of it all?*

What are you, the parent, getting out of homeschooling?

I've seen a lot of answers to this question – and the answers one parent (or other caregiver) has for this may differ from what their partner-in-parenting has for answers.

For example, I've just given you my list above. My husband's list as to what *he* gets out of homeschooling is going to include: a happier wife; the six kids he always wanted; the opportunity to teach them things (that counts as 'school'!) whenever he gets in the mood (I organize the rest); the flexibility to take us with him for work-travel; home-cooked meals; a relative lack of dealing with scheduling conflicts; and so on.

He'd have a lot of these benefits if I was a stay-at-home spouse and the kids were in school, of course, but let's be realistic – I had a paying career and probably wouldn't have stayed at home without kids. We certainly wouldn't have had *six* kids, because just the maternity leave and childcare – let along the driving them around later on that no pre-child parent ever really expects – would have been impossible. The Number One trait that predicts whether a university professor – like my husband – will get that coveted promotion to tenure? A stay-at-home spouse! Not to mention that we've all seen the studies that (happily) married people live longer. He can add a longer life-expectancy and his job status to the 'pro' list!

So... when my husband starts thinking about the huge financial hit we've taken (I've been home with the kids for twenty-one years) or the older cars we drive or our vastly-smaller-than-his-colleagues' house – he can weigh that against all these other things.

(And by the way, it's not just your co-parent with Opinions on all of this and with some investment in how you are raising your kids. My dad – who lives 1,000 miles away and homeschooled me and my ten-years-younger sister, as I mentioned – had a lot of anxiety about me 'giving up my career' to homeschool our kids. It was very stressful for me – but over the years it's become abundantly obvious that at least part of his concerns was about how he was seen in his community. When all his peers were saying "why isn't your daughter working in her field?" it felt like *he'd* failed as a parent. Now he hears a lot of admiration for our homeschooling and he's much happier. *He's* getting a feeling of success for having such rockin' grandkids and a daughter who is willing to 'give up so much' for the grandkids' success as his peers watch their own children and grandchildren and realize it's a crazier world than it was when we were all growing up.)

I know some homeschooling parents for whom the ability to travel – road-trips, or even world travel – is the defining thing that they get out of the experience. For others, it's the ability *not* to have to rush around – a more laidback pace to their lives is well-worth other hassles... and then there are the opposite ones who find that homeschooling allows them to pack *more* activities in than they could ever have managed to fit around a school schedule.

What your answers are to what makes it all worthwhile – for you as a person, not just for the kids – are going to be unique to you and your family. But, whether it's something as 'trivial' as sleeping in or as dramatic as visiting a new country every other month, these are real benefits that you-the-parent are obtaining from homeschooling.

It's easy to get trapped in all the 'don't haves' and 'can't dos' and forget that we have a lot of choices and that we need to own our choices. We have to own the consequences – intended and unintended – of our choices.

For example, my husband and I own the most boring vehicle ever – a ten-year-old white Chevy Express 15-passenger van that we got used. It's been

> **We have to own the consequences – intended and unintended – of our choices and of our "refusals to choose".**

shedding paint since we bought it. It's like a Soccer Mom Minivan on steroids (I was a gymnastics mom and I coach Lego teams... soccer was just a brief phase with us) and it gets *sixteen* miles to the gallon. We live out in the countryside – an hour from the city, as well as from most of our friends and activities – so, with gas prices taking off like rockets in 2022, I have to think about whether it's really worth the cost of driving somewhere. (We also own a ten-year-old Chevy Volt plug-in hybrid which my handsome husband takes to work every day... up to infinite mpg if we can drive it all on electric, which soothes my guilt over the van.)

Cool cars? Nuh-uh. New cars? Nope.

We're considering *upgrading* to a Soccer Mom car (a minivan) now that two kids are in college and we 'only' have to drive four around at once most of the time... can I get any un-cooler?

So I can look at all the *can'ts*: it's awkward to go out with friends (we're too far out even to carpool); going shopping for groceries is a Grand Process... let alone shopping for anything else; it's hard to park almost anywhere; I'm paying a ton to go anywhere; the back speakers haven't worked in years; we get high winds in this area a lot and high-profile vehicles like this get shoved harder by the wind; and it's a rear-wheel drive so we have to park at the bottom of our 1,000 foot hilly, twisty gravel driveway and trek down to the van on foot if it's icy... as we learned the hard way three times the first year we had this beast of a 'car.'

Or I can look at all the *cans*: each of my kids can sit by themselves (or enough by themselves) to seriously minimize 'he's touching me' fighting; I can – and have! – transported our entire Lego team, along with coaches, mentors, and some younger siblings as well as our two-piece 4'x8' competition practice board *and* a dolly to carry all of it; we can take extra 'junk' with us when we go on long trips instead of making choices that later lead to meltdowns (for one trip when we were dealing with a lot of food-pickiness I brought something like eight loaves of bread and ten boxes of three different kinds of cereal); it has a huge engine, so it cools down in summer and heats up in winter really fast; it's super reliable; we can carry home 4'x8' sheets of plywood for DIY home projects... or pretty much anything else we can imagine, like our hardshell kayak or large pieces of furniture (it's like a pickup with removable seats all the way back and a height limit); moving our oldest daughter in and out of her college dorm was a breeze; it has giant wheels, so we can go over anything... including the moderately bad flooding that occurs in our area on a regular basis; and it... kind of rocks to be the biggest thing on the road besides a semi or a fire engine.

And... we can always *unchoose* this vehicle if it becomes a bigger hassle than it's worth to us. We spent two years after our sixth child was born driving in two cars because we had a 7-passenger minivan that was paid off. It was a *different* hassle — and honestly, I'm torn about moving back to a minivan now that child number two is starting college because I like a lot of those features of having a 15-passenger van.

Homeschooling is just the vehicle we have chosen for our family.

If it unquestionably sucks for me to drive that van (and, yeah, I'm the one who drove it most until I got chauffeurs — I mean, kids with permits and licenses) then I should look for a better solution. If I feel miserable every time I think about getting in it (and it's high enough up that I had some foot injuries getting out for a while, so that actually was a thing) or avoid going places because I'd have to drive the van or find myself complaining about it all the time — or people not-so-subtly edging away from me when the topic of the van comes up — then it's time to find another solution.

The new solution may also suck in some ways: driving in two cars meant I couldn't ride with my husband and, in our pre-kids-who-can-drive days, that I couldn't do the read-alouds while we travel that we all love; it will mean that we'll have all those old problems when our daughters come home from college for breaks or visits; it will mean the Lego team needs other options; and it will mean a car-payment for a newer vehicle (instead of repair bills). No solution is perfect — but you do have choices about the ones you live with and the hassles you're willing to accept.

We did make some choices that are 'burned in' – like having six kids. And some that would be hard to re-orient from – like my twenty-plus year absence from out-of-the-home paid employment.

But homeschooling isn't one of those choices. It's relatively easy to unchoose it.

Which means it's a choice I make – and re-make – pretty much every day. Sometimes multiple times a day. (More on that in Chapter Two.)

And if I'm re-making that choice every day, there has got to be some pretty major reward in it for me... or I'll make a different one.

So how can you make sure you (and your co-parent) are actually getting some benefits for yourselves as people and as parents out of homeschooling?

TO DO list for figuring out what YOU need

- *Be honest with yourself about what makes you happy and fulfilled. Write a list and include minimum conditions – I need at least an uninterrupted hour per day to write or I'm going to be more frustrated than not writing at all.*

- *Ask your co-parent (or your child-rearing 'village members' if you're so lucky as to have more than one) to make up their list for what makes them happy and fulfilled.*

- *If your kids are old enough or mature enough – or you rely on them to help with house, siblings, etc – ask them to make lists as well. (These could be verbal lists or casual discussions...if asked, my kids usually each name one to three items that really matter to them and several of them hate to write.)*

- *Share your lists. It's helpful to know what everyone is thinking, and sometimes there's a simple fix, such as 'parent goes out on Tuesday to book club, other parent and oldest child will split cooking and bedtime chores'. My family decided to establish 1:30-2:30pm as Quiet Time for me to write (it expanded from there, but they've decided they all like the Quiet Time).*

- *If your co-parent (or kids) aren't really on-board with making lists and discussing things, it's possible to re-organize life to some extent 'on the sly.' More about that in upcoming chapters!*

  - *Don't accept a sucky situation. If you're unhappy – or your co-parent is – something is going to give. If that's the homeschooling and it improves your family's life, that's fine. But don't drop homeschooling unless that's going to be a fix for what's wrong!*

  - *And most important: REMEMBER! It's not just about everyone else. It's about you, too!*

Chapter Two

Why homeschooling 'fails' – or "why kids get sent 'back' to school"

WE'RE GOING TO START this chapter by thinking about how you have to choose – and re-choose – to homeschool every day. This isn't a situation where you can make the decision and then just go on auto-pilot thereafter... because you know that there is a public school just down the way that would be smugly, sympathetically delighted to have you show up and enroll your kids today.

Smugly because by coming to them, admitting 'defeat', you are proving their contention that education is better left to the pros.

Sympathetically because they know how hard it is to be around kids all day and teach them. Almost every adult in that building got a degree (or two or three) in education, after all. They've spent (or are spending) their time 'in the trenches.'

And delighted, because most of them genuinely feel a calling to help and teach kids and they are thrilled to be able to do that with yours.

As homeschoolers – regardless of our personal experience, or our kids' experiences – we should all be extremely supportive of schools and teachers. Just like us, they are doing their best, and if anyone knows and appreciates just how hard a job that is, it should be us. Not to mention that they are doing a good part of the work of raising our future sons- and daughters-in-law... and the people who will (hopefully) be working to cover our Social Security payments.

Sending the kid(s) to school, on the other hand, sort of *is* an 'auto-pilot' decision because everyone else does it. This is the path of least resistance, even if it's not the path of least effort for your particular family.

And no one tries homeschooling without making some serious lifestyle choices.

So, if that's the case, why do so many families give up on homeschooling within the first year, the first semester, even the first month? And for those hardy souls who push on past Year One, why do so many decide to send their kids to school in third or sixth or ninth grade particularly?

There are 4 big reasons, and we'll look at each of them in this chapter:

1. **It's too hard on the primary at-home parent/caregiver/ teacher, or on the family overall**
2. **We fear we are 'failing' our kids**
3. **The stuff they need to learn gets tougher as they get older**
4. **We aren't clear in our own minds about our goals**

Reason #1: It's too hard on the primary at-home parent, or on the family overall.

We've already looked at this reason in Chapter One in some detail.

I'll lump financial concerns under this issue – which we didn't discuss before because those are so specific to each family. If money is your primary reason for putting your kids back in school (or in school for the first time) then that's not an emotional decision: it's one of those hard choices that life throws at us and kudos to you for doing what you need to do to take care of your family. There are a lot of options that might let you continue homeschooling – from downsizing a home or getting rid of vehicles to moving in with parents or an elderly grandparent or even getting someone else to homeschool your kids – but those are *extremely* specific to each family. I've seen each of those things work well for some families and be disasters for others – know yourself, know your limits, do what's right for you and yours, and *don't feel guilty*.

In Chapter One we talked about how homeschooling should provide benefits to the parents – and how it *shouldn't* feel like someone sucking your soul out and running over it with a car. I gave you a few tips on how to begin to look at that problem: thinking about your cost-benefit trade-offs between homeschooling and public/private schooling; being aware that there is no solution that doesn't come with its own hassles; and being honest with yourself and your family about your needs and wants. It's very easy to get subsumed into What The Kids Need or What Is Best For The Kids and forget that there's at least one (and often more than one) adult in the picture and they have needs and dreams as well. A happy (or happier) primary at-home parent is likely to make it easier to solve other problems that arise – both with the homeschooling and with other family-based issues.

In the rest of this chapter we're going to look at the other three reasons why kids get sent 'back' to school.

It might (or might not) surprise you to hear that I consider Reason #4 to be the one that supersedes the others in importance.

Reason #2: We fear we are 'failing' our kids

The first thing to keep in mind is that if you are doing your honest best to meet your family's needs, *you aren't failing as a parent*. (And that 'honest best' may vary drastically from day to day. If you really are Supermom or Superdad all the time, you may have this part covered. I'm not, though! So, these are tips for us non-Kryptonians.)

A kid's needs are, in decreasing order of urgency (but not decreasing order of importance):

- Food, shelter, clothes, safety
- Love, understanding, time spent with parents, siblings, or other consistent caregivers
- Education and opportunities to explore their talents and interests
- Social opportunities (friends, coworkers, classmates), including jobs, sports, art classes, fieldtrips, etc.
- Respect and recognition from others and for self

We could argue about exactly where everything goes, and certainly the urgency of getting a job, for example, may rise as kids get older,

GROWTH POTENTIAL:
Learning

ESTEEM:
Respect, status, recognition, freedom

LOVE & BELONGING:
Friends, family, connection

SAFETY NEEDS:
Security, health, prosperity, resources

PHYSIOLOGICAL NEEDS:
Air, water, food, shelter, sleep, clothing

Maslow's Hierarchy of Needs
Each layer of needs needs to be met before the one above it can be addressed. The top level is where homeschooling takes place... but note that I called it LEARNING, not 'teaching' or 'education' or even 'homeschooling'. (The top layer is usually referred to as 'self-actualization': achievement of one's own potential... or the desire to do so.)

compared to spending time with their parents. I placed 'education and opportunities to explore their talents and interests' before 'social opportunities', but the traditional view as shown in Maslow's Hierarchy of Needs (see the first pyramid graphic) puts social opportunities at a more fundamental level and combines connection with family with social opportunities to connect outside the family. I also see Esteem as being derived from finding success at learning (the second pyramid graphic with the purple top).

However, the basic idea here is the same, whether you agree with me or with Maslow: that a given Need must be satisfied before it can serve as a solid foundation for the next level up.

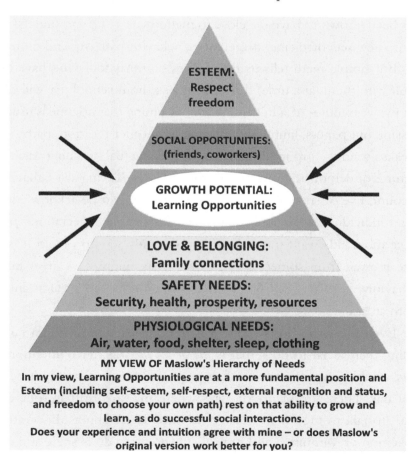

ESTEEM:
Respect
freedom

SOCIAL OPPORTUNITIES:
(friends, coworkers)

GROWTH POTENTIAL:
Learning Opportunities

LOVE & BELONGING:
Family connections

SAFETY NEEDS:
Security, health, prosperity, resources

PHYSIOLOGICAL NEEDS:
Air, water, food, shelter, sleep, clothing

MY VIEW OF Maslow's Hierarchy of Needs
In my view, Learning Opportunities are at a more fundamental position and Esteem (including self-esteem, self-respect, external recognition and status, and freedom to choose your own path) rest on that ability to grow and learn, as do successful social interactions.
Does your experience and intuition agree with mine – or does Maslow's original version work better for you?

It's often more physically laborious and time-consuming to meet a younger child's needs (glitter and glue cleanups and diapers, diapers, diapers come to mind). However, many – if not most – of a small child's problems are within the parent's purview to solve. Those first two categories above are pretty straightforward, and even if you end up with a child with Special Needs you have a great deal of control over the situation.

I know it may not feel that way... but fast forward to dealing with all the same things with your sixteen or twenty-year-old... Let's just say it's a good thing that their problems – or at least their physical size – often develop along with them. I have enormous respect for people who adopt – just having other kids over for a few hours or a sleepover has been known to have me close to meltdowns as I try to understand entire new sets of dietary preferences, behavior patterns, and more.

But simple math tells us that a class of thirty kids who have one adult with them (at a time) throughout a six-hour school day will each get twelve minutes of adult attention – assuming that no time is used in passing out papers, lining up, traveling to another location, bathroom breaks, waiting, group discipline, or even actual teaching such as lectures or demonstrations to the group at large. Taking all of that into account, five or six minutes a day where they might be acknowledged as an individual by an adult might be a reasonable expectation – and since most kids want more than that, the only way to obtain it is to take it away from someone else's five or six minutes. A great many behavioral issues are simply children starving for some real attention from an adult.

Even if all you do is spend a half hour listening to them talk – telling them what to do – that is *five or six times* as much attention as they would have gotten from their poor, overburdened schoolteacher that day. There are plenty of days where my kids drift in, one at a time, to talk to me for five or ten minutes. If it's about Minecraft or Pokémon or Vampirina all I'm probably going to do is smile and nod

– I know next to nothing about any of those things and really can't even make interesting or useful comments to show I'm listening. And we often end the interaction with me reminding them to brush their hair or wash the dishes or asking if they've done their math or writing. They roll their eyes or complain... but they had my full attention for those five or ten minutes and they know they can come back and have it again later if they need or want.

Some days that's all I have to give them... and then there are the other days where I have projects planned and everything organized and I *am* Supermom.

YOU ARE NOT FAILING as a parent so long as you are giving them the best YOU that you have to give them right then. That doesn't mean they won't end up in therapy or have strong opinions about how you should have done things differently. That's okay.

How many adults do you know who are replicating their parents' parenting style *exactly*? My husband said he'd have been happy to... but we've still done things differently – *he's* chosen to do things differently. That's not an indictment of his parents (they rock), nor are my different choices an indictment of my parents (they rock in different ways). Some of it is responding to today's different child-rearing environment. And some of it is realizing there probably were things that would have worked better for us if done differently.

And, yes, I've been in therapy on occasion, though nothing directly related to these parenting differences. There are things I do resent that my parents did – and probably some things my kids will eventually realize they resent that I'm doing. (And some that they resent right now that they'll later decide were good ideas in retrospect!)

My goal is for my kids to understand that *I* am a human, just like them. I will be both awesome and awful and I'm doing my best at any given time – and sometimes that 'best' is better than at other times. I want them to be tolerant of that – not just for my benefit, but so that they are easier on the other people around them and in their lives... and on themselves as well.

Humans screw up. We say we're sorry. We try to make amends. We do our best to make changes. We move on. And, probably, we screw up again. Hopefully in a different way.

Feed them, water them, give them a safe place to stay and clothes to wear, be as understanding as you can be... Those are the parts to get right – and to get help for as needed. The rest will come.

Reason #3: The stuff they need to learn gets tougher as they get older

So... we've dealt with the myth that we can fail our kids.

Now let's look at homeschooling specifically.

Of course people begin – or decide to stop – homeschooling for all manner of reasons and at all points in their children's lives, but parents seem to be *most* likely to homeschool through second or third grade and then put their kids in school. Conversely, other parents are likely to *start* homeschooling at second or third grade. The next point at which this sort of trade (some kids being sent to school and others being brought home) happens is in the first year or so of middle school, and then we again see the same thing happening at the start of high school.

Why?

It's actually the same set of issues in each case.

The parent either realizes there is a problem that they can't resolve with the school system and brings the kids home... or the homeschooling parent freaks out and decides they can't handle doing this any longer.

But why at those particular grades?

Simply put, those grades are when it feels like things have gotten substantially *harder*. Harder for us as homeschooling parents – or, if they are in school, substantially harder for our kids.

Kids in school who are moderately struggling, can find the academic jump at those points to be huge – and the parent with a kid going through that often notices that they are basically teaching all the subjects at home anyways (a practice called 'after-schooling'). Eventually it becomes clear that this might be less stressful if the kid was just home all day in the first place.

Bringing the child home solves the problem for the kid, but introduces new complications for the parent.

Most of us are reasonably confident that we can read, write, count, and do addition and subtraction. Second or third grade is when more advanced skills – like multiplication and long division and more detailed grammar – begin to be introduced in school. For many homeschooling parents who are following laid-out (bought) curricula this is a scary time because what the curricula are asking of the parent begins to get quite a bit more complex and time-consuming. Many

> **DEFINITION**
> **After-schooling: teaching your children while school is out. This can be either the stuff they are supposed to be learning in school or the stuff they – or you – wish they were. Many afterschool activities like scouts and music lessons might count as "after-schooling".**

(or even most) of us had positive memories of Kindergarten and first and second grades and so long as we can handle lots of cutting and pasting and keep coming up with tons of arts and craft projects, it seems we are 'doing the right things'.

The great news for parents *starting* homeschooling at the beginning (i.e., from Kindergarten or pre-school) is that there are zillions of camps and classes for kids of these ages. Most library systems offer completely free options, or an individual librarian who takes a shine to you and your kid(s) will often introduce an age-appropriate story-time or craft-hour and open it up to other homeschoolers. There are also a plethora of other parents willing to join you for playgroups, co-ops, outdoor learning 'explorations,' and more. It seems relatively easy to get help, in other words, up to about third grade.

Parents who are starting homeschooling at second or third grade are facing those more complex subjects head-on from the beginning, but the reduction in family stress that comes with not having to report to a school-teacher every day seems to help a great deal. The ability to take it slowly where needed and speed up in other subjects can transform the weekly (or daily) homework battles into something resembling a collaboration between parent and child... once an appropriate 'de-schooling' period has been completed.

'De-schooling' is a period of time where there isn't any direct attempt to 'catch-up' or 'skip ahead' or do any particularly formal learning. Learning is still taking place, of course, because *life* is learning, but it isn't being accomplished by force-feeding. The point of this break is for the child — but even more, the *parents* — to learn what it is like to be home all day together without anticipating that changing shortly. Sometimes this is about soothing separation anxieties that never quite settled out before, sometimes it's about learning where everyone's limits on sarcasm or joking around are, and sometimes it's about getting to know each other as people — big people and little people, but people.

> **DEFINITION**
> **De-schooling: a period of time where there isn't any direct attempt to 'catch-up' or 'skip ahead' or do any particularly formal learning. Recommendations are usually to take about one month per year of formal education that the child went through.**

De-schooling 101:
getting your new homeschool on track in the first place

Recommendations are usually to de-school for about one month per year of formal education that the child went through – and that is one reason why starting in second or third grade often makes a pretty smooth transition. Summer breaks of two to three months don't seem too crazy, whereas taking eight months to transition into homeschooling with an eighth-grader who is 'behind' academically can feel like way too much... but mostly because of the anxieties of everyone involved.

Don't be afraid to take the time you need to find that new balance – rushing this stage can lead to resentment and adversarial relationships. But don't feel bound by other people's 'rules' about how to do things; when you and your kid(s) are ready to start working together on a higher level of academic intensity, you'll know.

You'll know, because you'll see them start bringing you things that they are excited about (which could be an hour-long soliloquy on Minecraft – and my sympathies) or asking you questions about things they want to know (such as how long it takes NASA to send a radio-signal to the Mars Rover and get a picture back). This stage of de-schooling can be a little fragile because the tendency is to *pounce* on anything the kids come up with because – *at last!* But every homeschooling parent I've spoken to agrees that trying to turn every speckle of interest into a 'teachable moment' or 'taking over' the new interest is the fastest way to kill that interest. Answer their questions – or help them figure out how to answer those questions – but let them determine how far to take that interest. There is an excellent chance that the kids are (subconsciously) testing you to see if you are going to start force-feeding them academics again. Take these first flutters of enthusiasm for learning like the first flutters of a butterfly emerging from its chrysalis – as the delicate, easily disrupted things that they are. When an interest continues on with just a little assistance from you (you can help those fledgling wings dry out and unfold by providing a very gentle breeze) for a few weeks or a month – at that point you can get a little more involved.

And that's also the point where you can start insinuating a little bit of academics – gradually, not seven subjects for an hour each the next day. Start with the subject that naturally fits with the new interest – perhaps computer programming to go with Minecraft or a study of light and radio waves for the Mars Rover... or, conversely, ask them to write up the story of what's happening in their Minecraft world 'because it makes more sense to you when you can see it written down' or do some reading on Mars together for science. You can work a kid's interest into almost any 'subject' if you try... and if you don't call it 'English' or 'Social Studies' or (especially, even for the kids who are good at it) 'Math.'

PARENTS WHO ARE STARTING UP at this stage are often confronted with an almost overwhelming array of opportunities and a life made simpler by homeschooling. Some of the most ardent advocates of homeschooling that I know brought their kids home at these ages. These are the people who jump straight into starting (or joining) co-ops, organize 'class parties' for similar-aged kids, and create communities that fill the gaps in their social lives that were created by leaving their school communities. (Some of them are also the folks who just heave a sigh of relief and do their own thing... but they usually have their eye on what is available in the community and are seen at various activities.) To their delight, there are *also* camps and classes and scouting troupes and Lego teams and sports and many other activities available to these slightly older children.

But parents who began with homeschooling their toddlers often find that the new set of expectations as their children become eight or nine years old can feel overwhelming. The child whom you *know* can – or will eventually – read but *isn't* (or who *isn't* doing arithmetic or reading music or drawing or whatever the particular 'developmental milestone' they – or you – have hung up on) will make you question your every belief.

Some of my own kids started reading late – some *very* late (all the way up to ten years old) – and it was something I never expected, with both my husband and I having been 'early readers' (for the '70s). And you better believe that there was a lot of pressure to 'fix' this situation – this *kid*. Pressure from my parents, from well-meaning neighbors and extended family, pressure from my husband, pressure from other kids (unintentional, but kids talk about stuff) pressure from other homeschoolers... and pressure from myself. The one who took all the way until ten years old ended up being tested for ADHD, autism, dyslexia, poor eyesight... poor kid. The last thing I wanted was for him to feel there was something wrong with him... but it's hard to check for what might be real problems without doing just that.

Very luckily – for me – I'd watched a dear friend going through the same struggles with her daughter. My friend kept reading to her daughter and would type up this very creative little girl's stories for her. This went on until this child was ten or so and was reading and writing comfortably. I'm pleased to report that this girl is now a grown young lady who is working towards publishing her own written fiction! My friend's experience gave me the strength to stay patient and give my kid time,

Time and patience *work*. But man, are they scary.

(The rest of the story of my kid was that a great part of his problem was allergies. When we got those cleared up – and it took over a year, even with medical help – he went from reading "Go, Thomas, Go" to his little siblings because they loved to

> **DEFINITION**
> **Unschooling: an approach to education wherein the child is believed to have an inherent desire to learn. The parent's role is to provide an interesting and enriching environment and help the child explore their interests and meet their own goals.**

hear him do it and the short words were all he could focus on... to reading the "Wings of Fire" chapter book series by Tui Sutherland. It happened *literally* overnight because his sisters were reading it to him, but not fast enough. So, he got up one day at 5 a.m. and started reading. By 8 a.m. he had read three chapters – and from then on it was impossible to find him *without* a chapter book in his hands.)

There are lots of resources for parents who have been homeschooling up till third grade – including all those co-ops and activities being run by the new homeschoolers. There are curricula and online courses and the public librarians are just as friendly and helpful. But where once homeschooling seemed as easy as breathing and making breakfast, now there's a bit more effort involved. Even parents who Unschool find that they need to put more energy into finding things for kids to try or helping them delve deeper into the areas they are already interested in.

It's no great surprise – and definitely no shame! – that some people discover that public or private (or cottage) school is a great option for their family.

For homeschooling parents who are a little more confident of their academics, the big jump seems to be when the kids hit middle school or high school grades.

New opportunities for homeschoolers arise at each of those points, but they tend to have higher cost-of-entry, be less family-oriented (drop-off programs aren't always a boon if you have more than two or three kids needing to be in

> **DEFINITION**
> **Cottage School: a very small private school, often started by a homeschooler to teach other kids along with their own or begun as a co-op. Some cottage schools are run by (or become) larger private schools. Students attend 1-4 days a week, depending on the particular cottage school, and may be full-day or part-day.**

different places), and take more effort to locate. By high school ages especially, kids are specific in the things they need and want to study and how and with whom they are willing to do it – all of which can add up to a lot of extra effort for homeschooling parents who are already somewhat less than intrepid about this increasingly complex material. If we have chosen to use a curriculum – or are intimidated enough by the new material to try to find one, especially if we use Common Core or our state's standards for a guide – we may discover that we never learned some of the topics our children are now expected to know, not to mention that the Education System has changed how even things we did learn are taught in ways that don't make sense to our 'Old School' brains.

It takes a certain leap of faith to continue homeschooling through the middle and high school years. It takes realizing that you need to find your materials *á la carte* because the curriculum vendors with the "whole" or "boxed" curricula didn't know our kid when they were composing their excellent materials. It takes being willing to hunt for activities that fit your kid and your family. It takes being willing to keep seeking out and making new homeschooling friends – for yourself *and* your kid(s) – because some of the families you've been homeschooling beside for years have chosen school and they don't have time to get together very often anymore.

It takes being able to take the time to do all those things... and

> **DEFINITION**
> **"Whole" or "Boxed" curriculum: a set of textbooks, workbooks, lesson-plans, and often other supplies that are intended to fill all your needs for all subjects for one child for an entire grade-year.**

being able to keep living on one income even while the kid(s) *seem* to be more capable and independent. (Which they are, of course, but teenagers need parents with time for them at least as much as little kids do: the rates of teenage crime, drug-use, and pregnancy all speak to that. Homeschooled kids don't usually make their parents sweat over those things as much, due either to opportunity... or to having an adult around who listens when they talk and is clearly working towards their best interests even when they disagree about what those are. For many of us this alone is a reason to keep homeschooling through the high school years!)

And while money gets tighter, the supplies they need to homeschool with can be getting pricier.

I buy secondhand where I can, or try to pick items that can be re-used for several kids. (Perhaps this is why many homeschoolers have larger-than-average families!) Some things don't work like that – such as the cost to register my kids for their model government programs – and we have to examine our budget carefully every time. One good friend, a single-parent, has managed to homeschool her three kids – including a severely autistic child – up to or through high school, including having her eldest attend the same model government program on a scholarship. There's often a way... but finding it can take some extra effort – such as finding out about that scholarship and applying for it (or making the kid fill out the application).

While parenting little kids can sometimes feel isolating, *homeschooling* little kids tends to be very community-oriented if you want it to be. It's the middle school and high school years that can feel more isolating to the parent as the kids no longer are willing to play or hang out with your friends' kids and yet they still need so much of your time.

Sending the kids to school for middle or high school can be a sanity saver for parents who can't – or don't want to – keep putting that kind of investment of time and money into the homeschooling endeavor. There are trade-offs, of course, and the decision isn't irrevocable either way. The important thing is to choose what's right for the family – and not to be frightened off by "I can't" or "that material can't be learned at home."

Whether you and your kids choose to continue homeschooling or to have them attend middle or high school, own it! Pick what works for you, and allow yourselves to re-evaluate every semester or year (or every month, even) to make sure that it's still working and that you are all going in the direction you want to be going.

So... *continuing* homeschooling through the upper grades can be a challenge and you can choose to meet it in a variety of ways – and mix and match to find what works for your family.

On the other side of this equation are the parents who *begin* homeschooling at approximately third or sixth or ninth grade. Things aren't simple for parents with kids in school, which is why we see a lot of parents deciding to transition *into* homeschooling at the beginning of middle school and high school.

Many of these parents have recognized an insurmountable mismatch between the school system and their kid(s).

Some of these mismatches are developmental: puberty hits most kids somewhere between the sixth and ninth grades and a variety of issues can arise (or, if you're lucky, disappear). Kids also go through a major emotional developmental surge between eight and ten years of age, or right around third to fourth grade (referred to in some circles as the 'Nine Year Change'). By sixth or ninth grade – while they and their families are also suffering through puberty – many kids go through a surge of brain development and start to be more aware of their own post-academic goals and become a little more independent with mobility, bedtimes, and so on, which is also a huge and potentially stressful shift.

And some of these mismatches are structural – testing for Gifted programs and for some Special Needs isn't done by many schools until third grade, for example, and state-mandated standardized testing may begin around this age. It's possible, with time and money, to find outside experts to diagnose these additional needs and abilities, but it can be a challenge – as my parents found out – to convince a local school to work with you. Additionally, we break up K-12 education into elementary, middle, and high schools and add significantly different expectations to kids at those breakpoints – creating transitions which are based on age, but not necessarily ability or maturity.

I was brought home at the beginning of second grade after my mother (and my father, but mostly my mom, as he would tell you) spent *two years* trying to work with the school to find the right educational fit for me. Because the mismatch in my case was manifesting itself as migraine headaches, my parents had started with my pediatrician and then – on her recommendation – tried to look for an educational answer.

And, of course, there is no one-size-fits-all solution. Some schools are incredibly accommodating. My husband had understanding teachers pretty much all the way through and a pretty darn good educational experience. (Though, interestingly, his mother says if she'd known about homeschooling then, she'd have homeschooled him. Like my mom, she was one of the moms who volunteered in the school library and helped out with everything, running chess clubs and cub scouts... and doing a great deal of 'after-schooling'.) One of our friends had a very good experience with getting speech therapy for her son in the middle school years through our local, rural middle school – while other friends in the nearby large city school district have felt harassed and bullied by school officials when they sought similar help.

The middle school grades are also when kids begin sorting themselves out into a pecking order and bullying becomes much harder to control as Rosalind Wiseman famously described in her book *Queen Bees and Wannabees*. We've seen a wave of zero-tolerance school policies for the last twenty years or so, but the problem doesn't seem to be improving. We don't have to imagine the *Lord of the Flies* to be the natural state of children – a group of Tongan boys who were marooned for a year without adults on an island beginning in 1966 created a working democracy and cared for each other and all survived. The Tongan boys began by swearing a pact never to quarrel. In schools, however, kids face a different set of problems of survival and competition for adult attention; as we discussed earlier, there simply isn't enough adult attention to go around.

My ten-years-younger sister was brought home at the beginning of third grade because she was being bullied in a variety of ways that all managed to stay beneath the radar of a very caring teacher. It's simply impossible for one adult to keep track of *everything* that twenty to thirty children are doing, ensure that they are behaving humanely towards each other within the limits of their ages and abilities (teach them manners), give each of them enough attention to feed their starving souls, and also teach them all the content we expect them to cover. *Five or six minutes per day.* I don't mean to impugn school-teachers, who are trying to do far too much with far too few resources, but a homeschooling parent can provide more time and attention simply by having lunch or watching a video together.

Another concern for parents (and teachers) that arises at these ages – in part because of these developmental growth surges – is that a lot of kids become... *obstinate... difficult... mouthy...* Pick your favorite term. In the 1980s we called it snark – and it drove my 1950s era parents crazy.

It's another manifestation of kids testing out their independence, but it can be a handful to deal with. Or a few handfuls. It's very, very tempting to just send them to school and let the teachers handle it – after all, that's what they're paid to do, right? And they're trained how to cope with it, right?

Well, yes and no. An awful lot of teacher training is about surviving as a teacher within the bureaucracy of the Educational System and surprisingly little about handling smart-alecky kids. Not to mention that any given teacher has around thirty kids at once and if even a third are mouthy, it can be a mess.

I run FIRST Lego League teams – and I'm used to kids, obviously. Half the kids on the teams are usually mine. But doubling the number of kids I'm working with – for just two to four hours – usually knocks me out for the rest of the day. And these are all great kids – we all snark around with each other and have a good time. At least I have a parent there for each kid (or each set of kids from a family), so I'm not obliged to also be teaching them manners and refereeing kid-drama past a certain point (other than for my own). You couldn't pay me enough to teach in a regular school – and the gymnastics school my older daughters used to compete at actually tried to recruit me to teach Parent-Tot classes while my own kids were all in classes, so I can honestly say it's been tried.

Notably, there were only six Tongan boys marooned together.

And, honestly, if there had been even the kindliest, most understanding adult there their society would likely have gone off in another direction because that adult's attention would have been as scarce a resource as those that they needed to physically survive.

Between the work getting more complex and the kids getting snarky, there are definitely days when it seems much, much *easier... or better... or wiser...* to throw in the towel and let someone else have at. *Why am I doing this to myself again?* I cannot tell you the number of times I have told my kids that we are getting in the car and driving over to the school and registering them *right now...* I'm usually flummoxed in this dramatic pronouncement because it's inevitably past the end of the school day, late on Friday afternoon, or so close to the end of the school year that it just doesn't make sense.

Just as with Reason #2, Reason #3 really goes back to the first chapter.

Find a way to keep the primary at-home parent feeling like they aren't a martyr, but rather a <u>beneficiary</u> of the entire homeschooling enterprise.

On those "get in the car, we're registering you *right now"* days my kids know to make me eat some protein or chocolate or let me take a nap... It usually has to do with *me* being overwhelmed with too many scheduled appointments and activities, compounded with the kids fighting with each other or with me about 'school' work. On those days it feels like I haven't managed to teach them *manners,* let alone *math* – and we're back to Reason #2.

We've had far fewer of those days since the kids agreed to give me my writing time – and I started paying a little better attention to taking care of myself. Of course I feel guilty after getting all crazy and dramatic with them – and I feel guilty that they had to take care of me. But in the end, it's led them to be more compassionate with each other and with their friends – and better at emotional problem-solving for themselves as well. I'd like to have taught them those lessons a nicer way but...

Let me be super-clear here. I freak out like everyone else about my kids not learning the subject-matter I think they should learn when I think they should learn it. Or when my husband thinks they should learn it and gets on my case about it. He's a university professor who teaches engineering and my degrees are in biology. He had a minor in philosophy and comes from a very musical family. I had a minor in political science and am a dancer, artist and writer. Between the two of us we can teach almost any subject up to the college level – and a number of them past that. I like to joke that I went to college to become a homeschool mom.

Nonetheless, my kids are sometimes ahead... and sometimes very far behind compared to their public-schooled age-peers. And every single one of the kids has managed to 'fall in love' with a topic my husband and I still knew next to nothing about, even with all that prior preparation.

I'm a microbiologist and never studied (or cared about) insects and dinosaurs or sharks – so, of course, we have three kids obsessed with those topics. One child has been obsessed with cars from infancy – which is, again, related, but not anywhere near my husband's area of specialization in computer chips. Another is fanatic about history and Minecraft and gaming.

Keeping up with our kids' interests in order to find them Stuff to Do and Learn that they will care about – as well as finding ways to inspire them to learn the things we think they should know, like Math, English, and Science – has been a struggle for us also, even with all our 'preparation' and 'background'! And it definitely became more of a challenge around... third, sixth, and ninth grades – with *each* of them.

My mom, with her 1950s high school diploma, has so far done as well as my 'over-educated' husband and I. She sent two homeschooled kids to college and so have we. We're just keeping up...

Homeschooling life also became measurably easier for us as the kids became more alert to their own interests – and how to use Wikipedia and Google and the library. It became less of *my job* and more of a *collaboration with the kids* to find what works well. On the flip side, they also got a lot pickier about what 'projects' were worth their time and which groups they were willing to participate in.

What I'm getting at here is that the Problem is usually not actually the level that the kids are working at. The *Problem* is our *Perception* that we can't make it work out.

A detailed example on how it works out when you're helping your kids learn what YOU don't know

What I knew about cars before my son began indoctrinating me was... ridiculously minimal. I could change a tire, but I didn't even know I needed to change the transmission fluid. My husband knew *more* – my dad isn't a car guy, but his dad was the guy who kept the family's Honda Civic running by switching out parts with the dead one in the backyard. But neither my husband or I knew enough to sate our little guy's passion for cars with knowledge.

I'll even add that I don't particularly *care* about cars – I see them as transportation from place to place not to another (and better) plane of existence and delight as my son sees them. As mentioned before, we don't possess 'fun' cars. I don't think I've ever even sat in – much less driven – what my son would consider a 'fun' car.

Because of this son I've watched racing and can speak semi-intelligently about the different kinds of racing (but don't ask me about the specific series and cups). I can identify makes and models of higher end cars and (mostly) hold up my end of the discussion comparing where the engine might be located (front, middle, or rear) with more than noncommittal noises. Because this is our third child, everyone else has grown up with this – and his two older sisters as well as his three younger siblings can also discuss cars and appreciate them. Even the daughter who once said she never planned to own one is well educated about them (and may have changed her mind).

To help our son learn as much as he wanted (and needed) to about cars we had to search for people who knew more than us – a colleague who builds and races go-karts; the local mechanics to whom we took our vehicles for repairs; the husband of a homeschooling friend who drives a semi. We took our kids go-karting (totally new experience for me) and to the Corvette Museum (relatively local for us). Go-karting became a family experience that we now do a couple of times a year.

And as we looked for all these sorts of things, I discovered that my son was teaching himself Economics and Political Science and American History (and, more generally, modern history) through his fascination with cars. He gets frustrated with Physics and Math, but pushes himself through because he needs those subjects in order to understand cars in the level of depth that he wants to do. He was willing to learn to build and program Lego robots as part of our Lego team because it related to car control systems. He's even explored Biology to some extent by learning about crash-testing and the physical stresses that racecar drivers undergo.

While he was teaching me about cars – which turned out to be a lot more fun and interesting than I had imagined and *became* one of the benefits I get from homeschooling – I was able to nudge him into the subjects I wanted him to learn. He did it mostly without fighting (and this is a kid who won't do *anything* without deciding it for himself) because it was just elaborations of what he would choose to do anyways, or that he knows he needs for the dreams and goals that he's set for himself: racecar driver and automotive design engineer.

This is not to say he doesn't *fight*. The battles, however, are usually with himself and, so long as I can avoid taking them personally, I can be helpful and supportive and help him get past them. Math, for instance, has given us some very harrowing times. He's good at it, but he finds it dull no matter what curricula or approaches we've tried. Some things one just has to live with... but he appreciates that I tried my hardest to find a way that worked for him.

If this kid was in school – I can only imagine the battles we'd have had. Not to mention the fact that he's the one who didn't learn to read until age ten (and yes, I spent a lot of time very consciously *not* hyperventilating over that) due to that unusual manifestation of allergies. That late start hasn't held him back any... because of homeschooling. If he'd been in school... would he have been able to do AP Physics courses in ninth and tenth grade? Maybe, though those are often courses reserved for juniors and seniors...

But oh, those battles we'd have had to fight with the school, with him... with each other as my husband and I both tried to seek out the best way to help him with all that extra external pressure on us all.

If I can learn about cars and get this kid through high school... you can do something similar with yours.

IT'S NOT ABOUT THE LEVEL of the material. It's about the open-mindedness of the parent and the willingness to see what you are learning alongside your kid as one of your benefits of homeschooling.

You *can* cope with getting your child through more advanced material at home. The tricks are to (1) work with your child to understand their interests, passions, dreams and goals and view yourself as a facilitator to help them reach the place they want to get to; (2) use the things they are already interested in to help them cover the topics you – or the experts you've sought out in that field or area – have determined your kid will need to know in order to meet those goals and dreams; and finally (3) make sure you're aware of any local, state, or federal rules.

This doesn't have to be super-time-consuming. I have six kids, so if I spent a huge amount of time finding resources or cajoling my kids into trying new activities, I'd have no time for anything else. Certain times of the year (such as the beginning of a new schoolyear or semester) will necessarily require a bit more time spent. But mostly I find things by keeping my eyes and ears open throughout the year and remembering some of the things at useful times just well enough to be able to hunt down the parts I forgot. I probably spend a few hours every few months in tracking down resources – maybe a couple dozen hours over the course of the year.

Of course I can often then 'recycle' those resources by using them for a younger child... or by passing them on to another homeschooling friend or acquaintance. The homeschooling community tends to be very 'pay it forward': I pass on information about the opportunities I've found and delight in the things other people mention in passing, post on social media, or particularly bring to my attention.

It was actually a random social media posting asking for robotics mentors that ended up with my family becoming involved in Lego League... which we've been doing for fourteen years (with a few breaks). A friend casually mentioned that she was trying her daughter out in a homeschool gymnastics class – I asked for details so my then five-year-old eldest daughter could join her friend... the friend took classes for a month, but we just ended our relationship with gymnastics this month... fifteen years later with both my older daughters in college. We've found our model government programs through a random post from someone I vaguely knew as well – the coach has joked that our family has become the pipeline to finding people for her homeschool team because I promote and encourage others to join as well.

The opportunities that will excite and educate your older child are out there. They'll jump out at you at the most unexpected times. Grab them as the ones that are the best fit as they go by and do a little extra hunting for the things you know will particularly embellish their educational experience. And make sure you are having fun with it all, too!

I'm not only *wiser* than I was before I had kids, but I'm much more knowledgeable about all sorts of things from cars to baking bread to insects to the details of how our government works. I've learned things I never would have sought out on my own – and, honestly, things I sometimes would rather not know so much detail about. But I'm a better person for it.

The way I get through Reason #3 is by adopting the idea that I am in this homeschooling thing to educate *myself* as well. Try it!

Reason #4: We aren't clear in our own minds about our goals for homeschooling

This one is the biggie.

We often come to homeschooling from a problem-solving mindset. Our kid(s) has a problem that we can't see a way to solve within the Education System; or perhaps we see the System itself as the problem and don't want to spend all our time battling it instead of helping our kid(s) actually learn.

A problem-solving mindset is a good place to start.

But because we're often digging out from beneath a lot of mental baggage, we often don't sit down and actually, *explicitly* write out our goals for ourselves, our families... and our kids.

I tried polling homeschooling parents about this a few years ago on Facebook in a Homeschool Parent Support Group (Homeschool Parent Support Group-Louisville) which I ran, as well as in a group focused on Unschooling (Louisville Unschooling, Self-Directed, and Relaxed Homeschoolers). I was curious to see what kinds of endpoints the parents who were on these groups saw for their kids.

It turned out to be a useless exercise, because everyone got hung up on the Values Goals – we all want our kids to be happy, healthy, take care of themselves, be good people, etc. Of course we want those things for our kids. There are probably a handful of parents out there who would cross any one of those things off the list – perhaps in favor of some goal or ambition which seems more important than happiness (piousness, perhaps, or some particular achievement) – but I haven't actually run into any of them. We would probably all add a few of our own family's Values to that short list, but that's the core.

But let's be realistic.

When we were kids – or teens or adults – and imagined having kids, we had a picture in our head. For most of us, it was an image of them as babies. Even when you're pregnant or awaiting a baby to adopt it's hard to imagine them as a big kid, let alone as an adult with a spouse, a career, even kids of their own. Heck, I have a twenty-year-old and my fourteen-year-old is taller than me and sometimes I still have trouble imagining those things!

But, somewhere in that process of actually becoming a parent that changed. We saw them playing with dump trucks and imagined careers in construction and architecture. We saw them making play food and imagined them as a chef. We saw them watching the ants on the sidewalk intently and imagined them as an entomologist.

Some kids, of course, actually did have fascinations with specific topics that early on (my car-obsessed son made his interests known before he could sit up on his own), but for the most part these were our parent imaginations at work. Possibly we guided that early play into deeper interests. Perhaps we simply gave them lots of opportunities and gleefully observed their enthusiasms.

But we began to form a portrait in our minds of Who our child Is.

Of course we have expectations.

And combining those with that more extended list of family Values we end up with a set of expectations that are probably pretty detailed. If we don't face what those expectations are – and make them clear to our kids, along with where we are willing to give or compromise – we're headed for disappointment.

In the family I grew up in there was an expectation that my sister and I would study a STEM field and earn at least a Bachelor's degree. Likely a Master's. And possibly even a Ph.D. The arts were honored – but not as a serious career, despite the fact that our mother was a folklorist who knew by heart myths and legends from every nation in the United Nations and was also a professional folkdancer. (On her side, we are first generation college students.)

Our father, after all, has a Ph.D. in Electrical Engineering and we were Indian-American. Everyone we grew up around was an engineer or a doctor. One of the girls I grew up with – a 'wild child' who went off the beaten path and is now a professor of Archaeology – joked that her mother's family wouldn't speak to her if she didn't at least get a Master's degree, given that they were all doctors and lawyers. Except... it wasn't exactly a *joke*.

The expectations were very, very clear.

I got my B.S. in Biology and my M.S. in Bacterial Genetics. My sister – another 'wild child' – got a B.S. in Electrical Engineering and a simultaneous B.A. in Dance.

I'm a homeschooling mom – using all that education on my kids – and a writer and professional dancer. My sister is an engineer and manager at a large defense contractor... and still considering going back for a Master's degree, though she isn't sure in what field. (She's fascinated by dermatology and laundry and computer security and... whatever she does, she's going to rock it, because she learned early on how to set high expectations and define a path to meeting them.)

Were the expectations confining? Not exactly. They gave us direction – but we knew that our parents would love and support us no matter what. They would have been dismayed and concerned about our ability to support ourselves if we went in a different direction – but not ditched us. My parents nudged me to do something that would pay the bills – but they agreed to let me continue homeschooling through high school – *specifically* because my Indian engineer dad wanted to support my Writing! (As an example for gentle that nudge of direction was compared to others in our community who were following the 'traditional' school-based approach: while I was preparing to go to college to focus on Genetics as a more lucrative career option than Writing, a young man a year older than me – the son of my parents' friends – told me that *his* father had said *Genetics* was too iffy and he needed to aim for an M.D./Ph.D. program if he wanted to do Genetics... so that he could be paid as a doctor!)

We've also been very clear with our expectations for our kids. We tell them from early on that "McNamaras are problem-solvers" and that they are part of a team – our family. (My car-obsessed son got upset with this around age four and declared he was *not* a problem-solver... and then added that he was *not* a McNamara! I cracked up... because my four-year-old had just noticed that there was a logical problem in his statement – and then solved it!)

Our other expectations:

- that they will each either go to college *or* have another plan for when they reach 'graduation' age. (We're willing to be flexible about that age if someone needs another year or wants to be done a year early or something – homeschooling lets you do that!) We're *very* clear that starting a business, taking on an apprenticeship, joining a certification program, or a variety of other things that either support them or further their longer-term goals are all cool with us. Marriage would be fine also – again, with some sort of longer-term plan, but now for both our child and our child-in-law-to-be as a team.

- that they will not see honest work as beneath them if it's what is needed to earn a living for themselves or the family they have chosen to support.

- that they will contribute financially to and participate socially with *our* family after 'graduation' age if they continue to live with us past the time they would have otherwise gone to college. (This includes doing chores and attending family activities – which, of course, they are also welcome to do if they move out!)

- that we will help them with college or with developing and moving on with a different longer-term plan to the best of our financial abilities, energies, and taking into consideration our responsibilities to their siblings. (Our house is too small for people to move back home with spouses and children – but we have a big property, so they've been offered the opportunity to setup tents or yurts in the yard. I have also been clear that raising one generation is my limit, though I'll be helpful.)

- they will *complete* a college degree in any field once they have begun college. (The worst situation to be in is college-loans and no degree – but with *any* degree it's possible to work off the loans in a few years. My sister's Dance-major friends – after paying full tuition at an Ivy League university – were all debt-free within five years.)

- that it is OK to *change* their long-term plan as they go... but they should always have one while they are considering other options. "Look before you leap" is another motto for us... but so is "take the leap!"

- that they will complete a course in Calculus before graduating from our homeschool. (This is because this course is a baseline requirement for most STEM fields. The goal is a combination of both looking at their personal ambitions and my husband's statistical analysis with his department. Engineering students who get an A in first-semester calculus virtually always complete their degree. Those who fail first semester calculus or get Ds almost never do. Making sure our kids cover calculus before finishing high school means the *option* is open to them – regardless of whether they want to study Engineering, Economics or English Literature.)

- and... this one has sort of fallen a bit by the wayside, but I told them when they were small that they should each have a Sport, a Science, an Art, and a Craft that they love. To keep their body healthy, their mind stimulated, their soul inspired, and their hands creative. (And, you know, in case they have to rebuild civilization after they survive the zombie apocalypse. Thank you to authors Pamela Sargent, Sheri S. Tepper, and Ray Bradbury for this idea.)

GRANTED, SOME OF THESE OTHER things might flex a bit. So far we have one child in college and another (at this writing) about to start, with four more in the pipeline. Our kids haven't been particularly pro-active with the idea of dating – so we haven't been faced early on with some of the harder questions that might follow these things. At least one child struggles with depression – as have I, on and off. We are clearly not going to leave them to their own devices if they need a place to stay.

There are smaller goals, too, of course. Things like someone learning to take a shower all on their own, or finishing a particular math workbook, or even making it through a trying social (or educational) situation *that day* without a meltdown. Those are important, too. Without the small goals we can't reach the large ones – partly because they are steps to get to the big ones, and partly because we get discouraged along the way without some positive feedback on that longer path.

Interim goals bridge the gap between the tiny goals and the big ones. These can be things like getting a particular number or higher on some standardized test, being able to complete an entire outside class with a somewhat annoying teacher (or classmates), or finishing a big project like a book or even creating an impossibly elaborate Halloween costume.

But those are just our goals for our *kids*.

We have other goals for ourselves, of course. My husband and I have career goals, financial goals, even goals on where we want to live. I'm not a 'do or die' believer in visualization – but I am in clear goals.

The bottom line is that if you don't write out your goals, you won't *know* if you have a 'win' or a 'loss'. And that often results in categorizing your wins – sometimes even your BIG wins – as losses. Which makes you feel rotten and like a failure… and that attitude gets picked up by your kids, co-parent, friends, and extended family. Similarly, if you haven't written out your goals (big *and* small), you and your co-parent may view *one another's* wins as losses – or vice-versa.

Let's look at the nitty-gritty of homeschooling.

In addition to those big, end-of-the-game goals I just mentioned, we clearly have shorter-term goals for our kids, right?

Well, yes and no. At this point we consider ourselves 'unschoolers' or 'child-inspired' homeschoolers. What this means is that we don't stick to a particular curriculum and – as I described above with respect to my son's car-obsession, we use their interests to help guide them to reach the goals they choose for themselves. This works very well for us – and other people's mileage using this approach definitely varies – in part because my kids are extremely competitive. We even spent one year where I officially called us 'competition-based homeschoolers' and just had us bounce from Lego robotics competitions to Math competitions to Art competitions to gymnastics competitions and so on. We still do a fair amount of that (though that's no longer our 'official' approach) and now also have Essay and Oratorical (aka English) and model government competitions in our annual schedule.

But these are all things the kids *choose* to do. The support will be there if any one of my kids chooses participate, since other siblings are doing so, but we have had kids sit out any given competitions season in any particular year. It's not a problem... though since they usually have to tag along to the activity anyways it's often more fun to join in.

So, what kind of short-term goals can a family that considers itself 'unschoolers' even have?

Here are some of our current ones – and these have been arrived at as a negotiation between myself and my husband with tons of input from the kids:

- everyone does 'some' math and 'some' writing before using screens for entertainment. (How much 'some' is varies by age/ ability and what we're working on.)
- as kids grow older, more work-before-screens may be assigned.
- everyone should be at or above Common Core/State grade level in Math. (This is my responsibility to oversee.)
- no one is required to take part in a given competition, take a given exam, or join a given team; however, once you join, you are committed and required to compete or complete the season as appropriate, most particularly if dropping out will leave teammates high and dry. (We have a great many discussions about this as deadlines approach...)

- whatever you decide to do, you will put a full and enthusiastic effort towards accomplishing. The desired result isn't a particular score or grade or standing on a podium but to see how much you learned. 'Failure is not an option' because the only 'failure' is not learning anything.
- when mom or dad decide to do a project and call it 'school' you have to participate. (Usually this involves me doing read-alouds of Malcolm Gladwell books, such as *The Tipping Point* or *Outliers,* but most recently my husband has been taking everyone from the eighteen-year-old through the nine-year-old through a course in doing binary mathematics and computer logic.)
- we're all responsible for learning – and for helping others in the family learn
- we're all responsible for behaving kindly, a clean house, and making food – because we run our family as a democracy (Chapter Five) the rules around these issues have largely been generated by the kids.

THE GOALS WE WRITE OUT explicitly are the ones we develop a plan to attain. We end up creating specific benchmarks for most of them to be able to tell if we are progressing or have reached a 'win'. And we stand ready to adjust our goals as circumstances, interests and opportunities change.

The goals we leave unwritten (or at least unvocalized) remain as hopes, wishes, and dreams. We can't even tell if we have reached them, because we never give ourselves a clear enough picture of what we were reaching for. Worse, we may have multiple conflicting goals, or various family members may have conflicting goals that they don't even realize.

As an example, my oldest child began taking college courses as a dual-enrolled high schooler during her final year of homeschooling.

These courses were in what became her dual major when she went to college, so they were entirely worth it. In our state there are no requirements on what courses or topics a homeschooler must complete in order for their parent to declare them 'graduated' – and she was clearly ready. We had actually considered graduating her a year early and decided to wait so that she could improve her transcript with those college courses and try to get into universities like MIT (she ended up wait-listed there).

No requirements – but public schoolers in our state are required to take Biology. As we were homeschoolers it wasn't required (and in our state the homeschooling parents issue both the transcript and the diploma). But... I'm a Biologist. I talk about life sciences topics with the kids all the time, but I had been looking forwards to really being able to get into the details with my kids. And this one – my firstborn, my little girl – had moved to studying largely independently as it was for the previous couple of years. I was looking forwards to spending the time with her, reading and discussing all those things that were important to me. To make sure she covered the subject in sufficient detail, she decided to sign up to take the AP exam at the end of the year.

Her college courses had deadlines, though, and what she and I were doing could always get put off. First for this homework, then for that test. She was going to campus with her dad three days a week and I was feeling more and more left out.

In the end she got a 5 (the highest score) on the AP Biology exam.

But I still feel a bit cheated and disappointed that I didn't get a chance to spend the time with her that I'd hoped to do – and to delve deeper into some of the topics that I know she would have enjoyed more than just the basic survey course of introductory biology. What's worse is that the next two kids have had even less interest in Biology and I'm not sure I'll *ever* get to go over these topics with my kids.

I never really thought this goal out in detail before this experience. I never realized how much emotional attachment I had invested in this. I left off my career in Life Sciences in order to have my oldest daughter (or rather I left and then had her in short order) twenty years before, so it seemed like I maybe shouldn't care this much anymore. I don't *define* or *introduce* myself as a Biologist anymore...

But not writing out this goal – or at least verbalizing it explicitly to my daughter – made it impossible to meet.

I've seen other homeschooling friends do this with other topics... and end up just as baffled as to why the topic they *loved* and invested so much time, money, and emotion in flopped when they tried to present it to the kids.

I've seen others who put together what at least one of them called the 'Cadillac version' of homeschooling (in that case for one child) where there was a huge investment in time and money (seeking out and acquiring exotic resources and planning in detail how to use them). But they made their goals clear to the kid. In general, when the kid is 'sold' on the project – even if it's 'only' because they can see how important it is to their parent, the project will go well. My kids have all (mostly) learned to crotchet, knit, bake bread and cakes, do some embroidery, play competitive chess, program robots, do chemistry and physics experiments, play with unusual math, listened to tales of economic theory and parenting (we do some rather unusual read-alouds), paint, and draw... because one or another of them were humoring me at the time. Sometimes it wasn't something they came back to... and sometimes it turned into something they ended up loving and asking to do more of – or even pulling out to do on their own. Better yet, that "I'll humor them because they care about it" attitude carries over to their interactions with friends and siblings – everyone in our family knows more than the average about cars, insects, dinosaurs, physics, and math because those are some of our kids' obsessions. That respect and appreciation for other people's goals and dreams is one of the results of so much togetherness that seems a particular joy.

Sometimes a pre-made curriculum seems like it can stand in for writing out your own goals.

It doesn't.

The curriculum's goals may be explicit and detailed with lots of sub-goals and easy ways to tell if you are making 'wins'... but those aren't *your* goals or *your co-parent's* goals. Since the primary at-home parent is usually more involved in both choosing and using the curriculum, the other parent may not even be on-board with the actual goals that are being reached for. From their perspective it could be like shooting an archery target and getting a bullseye every time – but on the wrong target. From their perspective the 'win' *doesn't even count.*

Sharing Goals and 'Wins' in Order to Respect (or Reset) Other People's Expectations

I'VE SEEN THIS HAPPEN WITH numerous homeschooling families. Parent 1 is with the kids all day long and has their own set of concerns – often more about behavior. Parent 2 sees them at the end of the day – or the week – and doesn't understand the curricula being used well enough to make sense of what progress is being made during brief 'catch-up with us' discussions with Parent 1... which usually happen late in the evening or on the weekend when both are tired or busy. If you're lucky you have a helpful Grandparent or Friend or even a (step?) Parent 3 involved in your educational ecosystem – but that also means you have more people who have opinions and may be getting an even less clear picture of what is going on with the homeschooling. And all of these people have a set of expectations – frequently set by the snapshots they get of friends and co-workers bragging about their kids' best moments.

Even if everyone else supporting Parent 1 is supportive of homeschooling in concept, the picture they are getting is of a tired, frazzled, often-overwhelmed person trying desperately to cope and a kid or kids who aren't meeting unstated expectations. Since these are the people who care most deeply about you and your kids, they want to see both you and the kids happy and successful. Their suggestions may not always come across in a way that you see positively... but the less they understand your goals (and the less direct and extended contact they have with other people's 'perfect kids' or 'perfect families') the bigger a problem this is likely to be.

Conversely, the more time they spend with *you* and *your* kids, the better picture they are likely to have regarding your homeschool situation and to make more useful offers or suggestions. Keep in mind, however, that they will still see your situation through the filter of their own personality, background, and general perspective.

My dad is incredibly supportive of our homeschooling, but it wasn't until after we had our *sixth* child that he stopped campaigning for me to get a paying job – because he'd seen my mother's struggles to re-enter the workforce after my sister and I were grown. He couldn't see that I didn't have the time or energy with five children under the age of ten (though six under twelve apparently changed things); it took regular reminders from my wonderful husband that my dad was only trying to look out for me and reacting to my stressed-out state as well as my future earning potential to keep me from reacting... rather badly. Most of the time, anyways.

The other half of what changed my dad's suggestions was when he recovered with us after a heart attack and triple bypass, just before our sixth child was born. He had come out to help me when I developed debilitating anemia – and remember, my dad lives 1,000 miles away and usually only gets to see snapshots of our lives for a few days or a week during visits. That time, however, he got to see what it was like to be embedded in our lives. We started out with him giving me a *five-hour lecture* on how I lecture the kids too much (I was watching the clock) – and ended with him deciding I do an amazing job. He appreciated better how wonderful his grandkids are – but also what the challenges are of living and teaching them every day. My second son, whom I sometimes tease by calling him a kangaroo (he makes it across our small house in about three bounds), was the one my dad thought was 'most like him', but by the end of his recuperation period my dad was frustrated and worn out with this little boy's unending energy... he still loves my son, of course, but it was a window into my world that really helped my dad develop his perspective.

The three areas where the kid(s) missing unstated goals is likely to hit hardest and most repeatedly are: Math, English, and Performance Arts (including Sports). Why? Because these are the three areas where it's easiest to compare kids.

Of course it's easy to see that friends and cousins and co-workers aren't sharing all their kids' moments – they're sharing the best ones, just as you do when you're out with people who aren't part of your Inner Circle. The problem here is that we share entirely different things with our Inner Circle. They get to hear our moaning and groaning because we trust them to know it's occasional and not pervasive... or to be able to tell the difference and give you an outside perspective when you really do need to make a change (but not the rest of the time).

Unfortunately – or fortunately – the adults who care about you most hear a great deal of that moaning and groaning and they don't have a particularly deep understanding of what the kids are accomplishing. (Or perhaps that there is no such thing as a straight line for kids – remember all those Family Circus comic strips with the dotted line tracing Billy's way home when his mom calls him?) When that happens, these adults who care about you want to protect you – their child, friend, spouse, etc. – as well as help your kid(s). Sending the kids to school often seems like the quick-and-easy answer from their perspective.

If the person suggesting – or pressing – you to make that decision is also the kid(s) legal guardian, it can feel very hard not to cave... even though it really may not result in the trade-offs you'd prefer to choose.

Most times it's because the other person doesn't have a clear picture into your life. A dear friend of mine with three kids on the Asperger's spectrum felt a great deal of pressure from her parents to put her kids in school. Her parents lived a two-day drive away at the time and only saw her as a harried young mother for big family events or while they were traveling to visit. She could not get them to understand that working around her children's special needs also gave her the flexibility to let them grow and learn rapidly in the directions that they were ready – and let the other areas catch up as need be. It was exhausting, yes – but less exhausting than having to have meeting after meeting with school officials to sort out the problems and fit into the school system? Hard to say, but she needed her parents to respect her choices and they didn't always have her back the way she needed. Given the long distance between where she and her parents lived, it was a hard problem to solve – luckily her spouse had a clearer picture of the situation and was very supportive.

When it's your spouse/S.O. who isn't supportive, the problem can feel much more overwhelming.

My own clearest example of coping with an unsupportive spouse happened the year my oldest would have been in pre-K. We'd moved to my husband's new job some six months before. I had a four-year-old, a two-year-old, and an infant. I was still unpacking our stacks of boxes when I had a few minutes, but we had already found a homeschool playgroup that eventually evolved into a co-op, and we'd started attending those Waldorf Parent-Child classes. Senior moms (ones with older homeschooled kids, as well as our elderly neighbor with grown grandkids) seemed to think I was doing a good job. I was still looking for a family doctor, but we'd found a pediatric dentist already. I'm more of an introvert, so stretching out to meet new people while also dealing with three small children and setup a house was exhausting. Fun, but draining. And did I mention it was our *first* house?

My dear husband came home from work all excited one day. He had the answer to all the problems I didn't know we had. He'd been talking to his co-workers and discovered that the weird, post-integration school system in Louisville, KY (trust me, even the most enthusiastic proponents agree it's complex) had this amazing STEM magnet high school that he just knew our kids would love when they were old enough to attend. The thing was, that to get in you had to attend one of a handful of 'feeder' middle schools. And to get into *those* there were a specific set of 'feeder' elementaries. We had to get our four-year-old signed up for the 'right' Kindergarten next year! We had to do this right away!

And then he threw in the bamboozler: it would be for the *good of the family*.

I was so mad I could barely talk to him for about three days.

Finally, I sorted myself out and sat him down. He had this amazing new job, and he was getting a lot of positive feedback – kudos on his teaching, he even had a grant and a couple of grad students already. Of course there were setbacks, but he's a very positive (and a very ignore-it-till-it-goes-away) kind of guy, so he mostly shared the good stuff with me. He was clearly very happy and in a good place.

I asked him how he would feel if – after all of that – he came home one day and I told him I thought he needed to quit teaching and get a job in industry. For the *good of the family*.

He's a smart guy. He made the connection pretty much immediately. And he confessed that he thought I was doing a great job, too – he was just *worried about me* because he thought I was stressed.

Well, and I was, but rather moreso after his pronouncement.

I'd love to say we talked everything out from then on... but we're human. We still have unstated expectations and they come up and smack us in the noses every now and then.

When we moved to a more unschool-y approach (out of desperation, and more on that in Chapter Six) my husband was most definitely *not* on board. However, he agreed that he didn't see any great other options – by then we had a kid-situation that looked like it would only get worse in school. I knew that his unsatisfied expectations were going to be an ongoing problem, so I made a conscious effort to (1) have the kids show him what they'd gotten done or ask him a leading question that showed they were thinking about interesting things; (2) give him academic updates more regularly myself; and (3) save the moaning and groaning for my homeschooling friends instead of dumping it all on his shoulders.

Note, I didn't moan and groan to *my* parents or *his* parents – who are awesome, but personally invested in the outcomes. My friends were less invested in the academic outcomes for my kids and also were more aware that complaining that the kids were difficult today wasn't a sign of a chronic problem. People who are home all day long with their own kids have a different perspective – and even those (like my mom and mother-in-law) who *were* home all day long with their kids in the ancient of days of our childhoods have either forgotten or are seeing it through a different lens now that it's their baby instead of their bestie who's complaining.

For single parents – and I've known what I once would have considered a startling number of moms and dads who make this work – finding a way to bring your support system close enough to see and understand your and your kids' goals is probably even more critical. Even if you have a positive, pro-homeschooling relationship with the other parent you already know you a lot of points of friction to work out. One advantage that single parents *may* have is that a great many of their goals have had to be worked out and written down explicitly in a divorce decree or guardianship settlement – and if you are lucky enough to have a Friend of the Court or other third-party arbitrator who sees the value in homeschooling that can be useful as well.

Single homeschooling parents need those non-family supports – the ones whom you can trust to weigh in without having their own emotional investment in the situation – even more, however, and often have more hurdles of time, money, and babysitting to be able to reach out for that help. Other homeschoolers may be helpful in more than one of these respects, including having older children willing to babysit – or be a "parent's helper" watching the kids and even tutoring while the parent gets some work done without leaving the premises.

The single parents I have known – who ranged from a dad homeschooling three daughters after his wife passed due to cancer to several moms who needed healthier situations for themselves and their kids – have all had one thing in common. They have been very *creative* in finding ways to make their situations work in order. One wonderful woman with three kids – the middle one with severe enough Autism that he needs someone with him constantly – has used state-funded relief care to take classes to obtain certifications in a field she has always dreamed of pursuing. Another works four part-time jobs and self-employment options ranging from rating YouTube videos to sorting through batch-sold jewelry for unique or antique pieces to re-sell – her kids are very conversant in antiques

> **DEFINITION**
> Parent's helper: an older child who watches your kids, perhaps even tutoring them or helping them stay on task with schoolwork or chores, while you are present nearby and doing your own thing. They solve all the minor moment to moment problems, but you are there to handle anything big. A parent's helper is usually *cheaper* than a babysitter, and the job can be done by a somewhat younger child than you might feel comfortable with leaving alone with your kids... since you're still there.

pricing and appropriately (but not excessively) wary of internet videos. The dad with the three kids was a professional carpenter and involved his daughters in the business as they became old enough to be helpful.

When the kids clearly have some Issues that make homeschooling a better option for everyone involved – from Autism or ADHD to Diabetes to far-end Giftedness that makes regular classrooms a challenge for child, teacher, and peers – it can often actually be easier to acquire a team of supporters. When it's abundantly obvious that putting those kids in school would make it harder for you, your co-parent/spouse/S.O. as well as your parents and other emotionally invested individuals will often rally around the idea. When one of my children was having extreme temper-control issues it was painful for the whole family and I spent a lot of time crying – but sending him to school would have ended up labeling him with things that would be hard to escape and getting him put into the room for "bad kids"... pretty much ending his opportunities for learning as friends of mine who worked in those classrooms informed me. While we played with the idea of sending him to school – or all the others to give them a break from him – it didn't seem like it was a good idea. It would be bad for him, and since we honestly believed that we were affording more freedom and opportunity to our other children by homeschooling them, it wouldn't have been fair to them either. My support community – even those who might otherwise have been skeptical, like my parents and in-laws, or who felt a need to protect me from being overwhelmed, like my husband and parents – rallied. My local homeschooling friends were even more helpful in many ways, including putting Mary Sheedy Kurcinka's book *Raising Your Spirited Child* literally into my hands at a playgroup and telling me to read it *right now* and even coming over to my house one day to help me cope by cleaning for me and getting that closer-in view of our lives so that they could try to offer more pertinent advice. (I didn't actually *take* a lot of that advice, but it felt warming to know that they cared enough to try so hard.)

Other people's opinions aren't irrelevant to our lives – but sometimes they can be helpful as well.

How can you tell when you have a Homeschool WIN?

You can't until you've written out exactly what counts as a win. I'd even suggest posting it somewhere visible.

I've seen all of these things counted as wins by different homeschool parents – they're not all on my list (some have been), but they might be on yours:

- kid has a paying job by seventeen (… or 18, 19, 20…)
- kid can fill out a one-minute worksheet multiplication drill and get it 80% right
- kid is on grade-level for (subject X… each subject should be its own win!)
- kid has a steady job/S.O./graduated before starting their own family
- kid participates in a religious mission at the appropriate age
- kid takes a speaking role in a theater production
- kid is willing to participate in performance art in some capacity (including stage design, lighting, sound, costumes…)
- kid makes it through a co-op or playgroup (for their siblings) without a meltdown
- kid can cook a full meal
- kid can plan *and* cook the meal
- kid starts a business
- kid actually makes money with their business
- kid has a friend
- kid spends more than two hours (cumulative) outside their room on a given day

Yeah... some of these goals are pretty basic. Sometimes our *needs* for what has to happen to count as progress is pretty basic. The parent dealing with a toddler or two might to count eating broccoli as a win – the parent with the teenager is facing different issues (and maybe also the broccoli thing).

It's important to count *all* the wins. Because it is so much easier to wallow in the 'fails' (but remember, there *are* no failures – only learning opportunities that got a little messy along the way).

TO DO List before putting the kids back in school

- Write out your goals for your kids, especially, but not only the academic ones

- If your co-parent or kids or other invested parties will write out lists, ask them to do so

- Compare lists: do you need to combine all the lists into a Family Super List? Are there smaller goals that will give you more 'wins' per unit time? Does everyone agree on the Bigger (or longer-term) goals?

- Consider posting your list of "What Counts as a Homeschooling Win" up on your refrigerator (or some slightly less busy but still visible) space.

- Track your wins – and celebrate them! Even small things can be an excuse for ice cream or high fives.

- Keep sharing your wins with your co-parent and other invested parties. Do it where the kids can hear – it's inevitable that they hear what didn't work when we grade or correct their work, so a bit of positive feedback (both directly to them and where they can hear you telling others) is fully warranted.

- Remember:THERE ARE NO FAILURES (only opportunities to learn something we maybe didn't plan on)

- ...and that includes sending the kids to school. If that's the right decision, do it. But don't do it because of thinking you can't handle the work or that your kids will end up in therapy later. Do what feels right, keep your 'Village' on board, and enjoy the journey.

Chapter Three

Stressing Out is for Other People
(but so is a clean house)

"SURELY YOU JEST," SAY YOU on reading that title. "Surely I can have both!"

Perhaps you can. I won't deny that I have seen some absolutely Martha Stewart Magazine-ready homeschooling homes. You can find beautiful pictures of people's 'homeschool rooms' all over Facebook groups: a quick Google search got me pages and pages of pristine, lovely rooms filled with neatly shelved books and papers in folders... Desks and tables and chairs that are empty to be sat upon and...

I do wonder how long the rooms took to be photo-ready and how much had to be cropped.

On the other hand, I *know* people who actually homeschool in that kind of environment... so I know they are somehow *real* and not mythological (or sneaky with their photo editing).

I envy those people. I really do.

I grew up as the daughter (and granddaughter, and *great-*granddaughter) of a hoarder. I'd like to think I'm better about throwing stuff away than my mom – and that it's just that I have a tiny house over-filled with kids – but you can probably hear my husband laughing in the background, even through your eReader or paperback.

I claim that my housekeeping skills are really quite good after all these years – it's just that the kids always manage to stay ahead of me. We'll find out as they grow up and move out, I suppose, so I have another nine years before push comes to shove. (Or longer – the nine-year-old is in the 'I am never leaving you' stage, and her current lifeplan is to be a professional unicorn finder. Which can be done from our house, because unicorns are 'where you don't expect to find them'. We've all attempted to debate this logic, since she clearly *does* expect to find them here...)

I homeschool (I homeschool)
I'm sane, too (I'm sane, too)
But there ain't no way I'm gonna have a clean house
Don't be mad...
'Cause two out of three ain't bad...

(with apologies to the memory of Meat Loaf)

ALL JOKING ASIDE, MY MENTAL health and the kids' academic progression (and their mental health) comes before the clean house. And since I can't afford to pay someone else to clean right now (and, oh goodness, the *pre*-cleaning because things are *everywhere*) is just not happening. Not to mention that – hello? I have five kids at home. (But we'll talk about chores and responsibilities in Chapter Five)

We don't have a homeschool room – and the kids don't even have desks. This is partly because we have eight (seven now that the oldest is away at college 93% of the time) people living in fifteen hundred square feet. We use folding tables and chairs – which often become 'temporarily permanent' fixtures while a project is going on or a game is being played for multiple days in a row or... whatever. We suffer from 'surface hemisphericity' – the tendency to turn every horizontal surface into a mound that becomes somewhat hemispherical.

And, yes, we fight back against this.

With regards to floors, for example, my mother-in-law gave us a Roomba

> **DEFINITION**
> **Surface hemisphericity: the tendency to turn every horizontal surface into a mound that becomes somewhat hemispherical.**

back when the kids were little. They named it Rudolph for the red light on it, and Rudolph introduced us to the concept of multi-level cleaning. There was 'mom-clean' – where I would vacuum, stopping to save everything including Barbie shoes and those itty-bitty, single-peg, clear, round Legos, and then I'd dump the bagless vacuum out in a corner of the backyard so that later, after some rain, the kids could find the precious items I'd missed. There was 'Daddy-clean' – he'd still stop to pick *some* stuff up, but if it's gone it's gone. And then there was 'Rudolph-clean' – because a robot vacuum cleaner doesn't save *anything*.

There was also 'playgroup clean' – meaning I could bear to have our playgroup over – and 'grandparents clean', which was much more intense. For far too many years our Lego teams met in our house – which required much more regular cleaning to make work. I loved the cleaner house, but hated how stressed it made me to get it that way and the amount of yelling and weeping involved. (Those were usually both on my part, just to be clear – first yelling and then guilty weeping because I'd yelled... and because the house was still a 'disaster' despite all of that.)

If you have space to be organized or you are a calmer person – the clean house thing may work for you.

If you are less attached to Things, it may also work – though minimalist homeschooling is... kind of a pipedream. If the curriculum vendors don't get you, the kids will fill in by being three-dimensionally creative.

Some things simply have to stay. My silly husband suggested a year or so ago that we could get rid of some books (most of our many books are double-shelved) – and I was very pleased when all the kids stared at him in disbelief. I *did* box up a bunch of the younger children's books – to store for future grandchildren, thank you very much, because they'll be out-of-print by then – but my suggestion was to get rid of the kids instead. I mean, that's already happening – we have a couple more or less out the door – so then we'll have more space for the books. It was hilarious to see his expression when the kids agreed!

We all have to make choices in our lives about what stays and what goes. For people like me – whose hoarding tendencies might be blamed on either nature or nurture – it's hard. And I *do* get rid of stuff.

But I don't want to end up in the situation of a girl I tutored in college who threw her Physics notes away – *halfway through the semester.* She had no idea what she'd studied because she'd decided to tidy up too soon.

What to Save and How

Figuring out what to keep – and how to store what must be kept – is important. Digital files are great for making that easier, of course, especially for long-term storage. Some homeschoolers take pics and videos of everything they do and then ditch the originals. If you try this, just be sure you back everything up in more than one location! We all have to be able to show the kids' recent work if the School District or Child Protective Services comes calling (which seems to happen to about every other family – homeschooling or not – when some neighbor gets in a snit), so there's something to be said for keeping at least the last six months' or year's productions where you can lay hands on them physically.

What if the School District checks on us?

This is the big fear, right?

The first, and most important thing to note is that this is *EXTREMELY UNLIKELY.* School district officials have tens to hundreds of thousands of kids who are enrolled in their schools to keep track of and provide services to – randomly checking on local homeschoolers is usually not even on their radar.

The cases where the school district (or Child Protective Services) calls a homeschooler out almost always have to do with a report – often an anonymous one – from a disgruntled family member, friend or neighbor. And since YOU are doing everything within the rules of your state, it's an annoyance not the end of the world. Though it can feel like it when it happens, since you are *literally* being judged on your parenting. Certainly *I* felt judged when it happened to us... even though the problem went away almost instantly and the CPS social worker actually said it was nice to visit a family where nothing was wrong.

So... first thing, make sure you know what laws you are homeschooling under. Look at the *actual* laws, not just some other homeschooling parent's summary of them. Make sure you are in compliance with those laws.

And it will all be fine.

Personally, I don't (gasp!) keep *every precious scribble* – but I do keep quite a bit. I've found that a given kid generates a thickness of ¼" - 2" of 8 ½ x 11" papers worth saving each year... and it's usually more in the ¼" - ½" range. (The usual items that increase the thickness are completed workbooks – which I often store elsewhere ultimately – and awards and certifications.) Everything goes into a hanging file folder – one per kid – through the year, and then move it all into a 10"x13" manila envelope (the kind with the string or metal tabs so they can be opened and closed multiple times) before we start our new schoolyear. One smallish plastic box with moisture seals holds two years of six kids – or 12 years' worth of one kid... which really isn't that much to store. Because I use boxes with moisture-seals, we can store them in a barn/garage/basement without worrying about climate-control. (I use Ziploc 16 quart/4-gallon WeatherShield Storage boxes: 17.43" x 11.81" x 6.69". For comparison, this is about somewhat less volume than a rolled-up yoga mat.)

What do you *need* to save?

That would be, first of all, anything that your state requires you to present as documentation of your homeschooling.

For states – like New York, California, Virginia, and so on – that have very detailed requirements of homeschoolers, please follow the rules. If your inclination is to Unschool and the regulations seem too restrictive, contact your state Unschooling organization (find them online, every state seems to have one – if you have trouble finding yours, ask in neighboring states or look for local groups) and find out how those parents are doing things already. If you choose not to follow the rules and take your chances – knowing that school district officials are usually too concerned with the very real problems of the students already enrolled with them (including food insecurity, homelessness, and domestic concerns – in the large urban school district we live adjacent to, these issues involve some 20-30% of the 100,000 kids that the district is responsible for... and last I heard they had less than

25 district employees trying to help all those kids) – then please, *please* know what you are getting into.

I recommend following *all* laws regarding homeschooling: if you think the laws are wrongheaded, teach your kids a unit on citizenship and work to get those laws changed!

For states that aren't very specific, like Kentucky and Indiana – or only require you to show what you've been doing in the *extremely* unlikely event they decide to check up on you – make sure you have an example of *recent* work in every subject area for each child; this can include awards, certificates, pictures taken of work that you counted for that subject (say of a garden or a Balsa bridge or a robot or a chicken coop).

Legislators and school districts try to shoehorn homeschoolers into the boxes they already have to check off, so they often ask for *attendance*. This is often seen as the most nonsensical of requirements to homeschoolers: the kids were here today; they were here yesterday; they'll be here tomorrow (I can't get rid of them if I try). Since it seems so insane, we often try to make it seem more complex than it is. I'm not aware of any state that requires kids to be performing "schoolwork" during certain specific hours so long as the total number of days and hours set by law is met. Most of these less-regulated state school district officials don't want an hour-by-hour accounting if they end up having to audit – they want to see a list of days and are frequently satisfied with a calendar where dates have been checked off. A nice touch could include a running total – to show when you've reached as many days as you need to be able to report. I wouldn't include a list of topics covered on a given day unless that information is specifically requested... but you should be able to put that sort of thing together in a few days if requested.

Also remember: you can *and should* request to schedule a meeting 3-5 days hence if the school district contacts you regarding your homeschooling. In many states homeschoolers are actually considered private schools and the parents are the principals or school administrators. Such people's time is precious (as is yours) and it wouldn't be expected that they could and should drop all their other work suddenly (nor should you). If they show on your doorstep instead of properly contacting you by a letter on letterhead, you can offer to schedule a meeting.

You also never need to let school district officials or even social workers from CPS into your home. This works better with the school district – CPS will be back with a police officer and a warrant and possibly a bit more adversarial attitude. But keep in mind: these people – both social workers and school district – are responding to a report that there is a concern for the welfare of your children. It sucks when it happens to you, but after speaking to many, many parents – both homeschooling and not, as well as a homeschooling parent who actually *was* a CPS social worker – I've come to the conclusion that CPS is really easy to deal with so long as your home is reasonably clean and your kids are reasonably happy and clearly learning *something*. Remember, they see the really bad situations... and they're aware that a family that is homeschooling is one that is putting extra effort into their kids. I haven't personally had to deal with school district officials in this way, but the people whom I have spoken to – including the mom who was badly harassed by a new hire in the department – agreed that the problem went away quickly once they showed some of what their kids were doing. Both sets of people want to get back to their jobs of finding and helping the kids who really *are* in dire situations – few of them have the time to bug hardworking homeschooling parents.

That's especially true in large, urban school districts, of course. In rural areas you may find a different approach – which could be either *more* or *less* friendly and largely depends on the personal biases of the local officials rather than broader policies.

In summary: keep the last year's worth of your kids' work (or anything that demonstrates what they have accomplished) where you can lay hands on it easily. If you have a "feisty" neighbor or a disagreeable ex-spouse, hold onto at least the last *three* years so you can quickly demonstrate to anyone (including worried grandparents) how much progress your kids have made.

The rest of the stuff you hold onto is for sentimental value. When my kids settle into their own adult lives, I intend to hand them each one of those small plastic boxes with all the "records" I have from their homeschooling years. It will be something to look through and set aside... and maybe show their own kids someday.

Setting Priorities

But what sorts of things to hold onto is just details, really.

Keeping my sanity and keeping the kids moving forwards is much more about broader strokes.

It's about deciding whether home-cooked meals are a top priority this week – and sometimes they are, such as when we were checking for allergies... and then for several years thereafter when we found that we had to avoid all oils used in fast-food (thank goodness that one was outgrown).

It's about deciding whether listening to my teenager for five hours straight as he works through his existential crisis (in multiple repeats) is more valuable than sweeping the living room. Or picking up in order to sweep.

It's about realizing that although I have six kids, and my friends with one or two seem to average six activities *per* kid – that would utterly kill me. My kids and I work together to decide which opportunities and activities are worth it – cost and time of travel (remember we live an hour away from most things and everyone hates sitting in the car just to turn around and go home after dropping off one or two siblings) are weighed versus the fun and learning and social opportunities that we want.

I've been known to jump through some crazy hoops to get everyone everywhere... but it tends to make me a crazy woman and no one enjoys that.

COPING with busy schedules

One of my coping techniques is to talk several of them into doing the same activity. All the kids in our family have done gymnastics because the older girls were competitive gymnasts (and then coaches, so the younger kids got a discount on classes). All of my boys do archery and all four younger ones did indoor soccer for a while. Two of them did a summer-long gardening class together. Everyone has to agree on the playgroups or co-ops we attend – or be old enough to stay home, or find a sibling old enough to watch them at home. (A variation of this keeps me from busting my clothing budget: they can usually talk me into nicer/fancier clothes if they get buy-in from the next one in the hand-me-down list, or certain toys if they can persuade a sibling or two to also campaign... Though this only works until they finish growing.)

Another coping technique has been to run the activity myself so I have control over cost, location, and scheduling. While this isn't always feasible, it can work better for scheduling a large family than trying to puzzle-piece together other activities. All of my kids have participated in Lego teams because we were running them (at our house until the last few years) and they were going to be there anyways; they could entertain themselves or they could be on the team. I've had kids make either choice in different years.

I'd like to distinguish here between 'sane' and 'calm' or 'patient'.

For me *'sane'* is *'not rolling around on the floor in excruciating abdominal pain because I'm overwhelmed'*. When I start to reach that point, I know it's time to back off (hopefully a little before that, actually). For ten years or so, one of my kids was our 'bellwether' instead – he'd have meltdowns when our life got too busy and I never hit *my* limit because I was watching to keep *him* from reaching *his*. (This also worked to keep me from getting hypoglycemic and faint – if you have to feed a bunch of kids four or five times a day you never hit a 'Snickers' moment.) As his limits stretched and he became more able to cope... I've ended up more prone to pushing mine.

'Calm' and *'patient'* are a whole 'nother matter.

We frequently run into people – in grocery stores, at parties, on the street – who are amazed that I have six kids and homeschool. The reaction is usually "oh, I'd love to do that, but I just couldn't handle it. You must be so patient."

My kids... are not even subtle about it. They simply start guffawing.

I am not calm when I am excited about something. I wouldn't go so far as to say I am a high-strung person, but when something is important... well, let's say I am *passionate*.

The patience thing isn't really fair, though. When I get *passionate* about someone picking up their room or finishing their math for the day after the fifth (or fifteenth) gentle reminder... that's still pretty darned *patient* in my book. And, honestly, in my kids' books as well. (My husband thinks I am *too* 'patient' in regards to picking up their rooms.)

We've found some tools to improve my *calm* and *patience* – which I'll tell you about in Chapters Four and Five (when we talk about finding parent-based social opportunities as a homeschooler and dealing with chores, respectively). But the important message to carry away here is that the kids will be okay with some level of *passion* and, erm, *enthusiasm for getting things done right now*. What that exact level that is okay will vary from family to family and kid to kid (and don't forget that your spouse or co-parent's tolerance may be at a different set-point) but a little yelling isn't the end of the world. It doesn't make you a contender for World's Worst Mom/Dad. It just makes you human.

My kids are actually much more concerned when Daddy is mad about something because they don't know what to expect from a man who is very rarely angry. With me, they know it's all summer showers – thunder, lightning, a bunch of rain – and then sunshine again. With him... they all tiptoe until they figure out what's up.

There's actually something to be said for developing a kid's tolerance for different personal styles. We don't know what kinds of people they'll end up interacting with and getting them to see and understand the difference between *effusive* and *abusive* may be an important life skill – not only to protect them from others, but also so that they can see what will be the most effective methods of communication. For example, a friend of mine who grew up in a very Right-Wing household was stunned the first time she listened to NPR: *"don't any of these people care about the topics they're discussing?"* she wondered, since she was used to the more bombastic and impassioned approaches heard from broadcasters like Rush Limbaugh. (My mom taught me this idea in a different context when our oldest was born – she said "don't tiptoe around when she's sleeping or you'll be doing that for the next ten or twenty years – let her get used to some noise!")

Pick Your Battles

Bottomline?

Pick your battles.

If a clean house or home-cooked meals or serving at church or participating in Scouts or being the Team-Parent (who plans parties and organizes snacks and gifts for the coaches) is important for your sanity – then do it. Just don't try to do *all* of those things *at once*.

If you're choosing to homeschool, then you're choosing to have half-done projects spread out *somewhere* at least 90% of the time. If you have a homeschool room you *might* be able to confine the projects to that space... depending on your kids, their projects, whether you want to bring in drills or glue or water or whatever... And depending on whether you are willing to enforce 'school in the school-space' rules.

My husband and I are entirely on the same page that learning is a lifelong mission – as you might guess with him being a professor and us homeschooling. We might *like* a cleaner house (okay, I *know* he would) but we don't like the idea of confining our kids' projects and learning to any particular space – or time.

We 'school' around the week and around the year, though for shorter hours most days than many others. We talk about science and books and news and history and art and movies... and argue about which version of The Flash (from the DC TV series) is the fastest superhero/villain. I write my books in my bed so I can arrange my ergonomic keyboard just right with blankets to angle it – or sitting under the window air-conditioner that the kids helped re-install for the current heat-wave – or standing at the kitchen counter when I try to get serious about losing weight ('never sit if you can stand'... hah!). My husband curls up in bed or in a chair to play online chess or grade papers or play Civilization IV on the computer with a kid or two kibbitzing over his shoulder on strategy and historical accuracy. We read books as a family that will make us argue and end up having deep moral and philosophical discussions after watching Disney Princess films and Marvel movies because we think that's fun. (We also have tried pretty much every sport we can get our hands on – we're jocks *and* geeks *and* nerds, thank you very much!)

And when it comes down to it, I'd rather argue with my kids for two hours about whether Thanos' goal of population control was valid (we all agree that his method – wiping out half of all life with a snap of the fingers – was both morally reprehensible *and* pointless, given population curves) than scrub my sink.

Sorry, Fly Lady! (www.flylady.com)

It's the 'twenty years' test. In twenty years will that shiny sink today make a difference? Or will the argument that was so much more fun?

If we're all going to get food poisoning and die from the dirty sink... or if I'm going to yell about the sink or stress over the sink...

Then it might be the sink.

It's my *choice* to make — each day and each time I can clean (or run a meeting or a team or drive across town or...) or choose to spend time with my kids (or writing a book).

TO DO Sanity Savers

- *More lists: what is siphoning gas out of your emotional car right now?*

- *Remember the lessons of Covid-19 and all those 'critical' activities that turned out to be a relief when they were canceled. Did you add them back in automatically when lockdowns lifted and people started getting back together? Be intentional in what you choose to fill your life with.*

- *Remember the other lessons of COVID-19: stay clean, but clean the things that matter. Disinfecting our groceries was overkill for most of us once we found out it wasn't touch-transmissible, but washing our hands reduced the flu and headcold numbers as well.*

- *Your kids will be fine if they do one or two activities a week or even a semester. Even the extraverts may prefer not to be out every day if it means a happier at-home parent (this is what my flaming extravert kids tell me).*

Chapter Four

Raising Adults, not Kids
(or "What about socialization?")

THAT'S THE GOAL, RIGHT?

Even for those of us who can imagine a life where our kid(s) live with us in a multi-generational household for the rest of their – and our – lives, we expect they'll grow up. After all, someday *we'll* be the ones needing our food cut up and our laundry done, and *they'll* have to be the ones doing that... or making sure someone else is paid to do it.

As a homeschooling parent you have a special opportunity to connect with your kids as they grow up into adults. You'll be with them more, so they'll see you living your values... or not. They'll see you on your good days and your bad days – and there *will* be bad days. You can't just put on a happy face when you're with someone 24-7 and they try to talk to you while you're using the bathroom right after your mom (or dad or S.O. or best friend or boss...) told you that you should quit homeschooling (or coaching a team or doing that much volunteer work...) because then you could be a *happier parent* and that's *better for the kids*. I also defy any parent to respond rationally to a sibling screaming match over who had to use the other blue crayon or questions about math or a soliloquy about Minecraft while the parent is having their own existential crisis or "communing" with the "Porcelain God" after a bad taco.

Your kids are going to see you as a human.

That can be good or bad, depending on how you see it. If you want to be the all-knowing parent... that's a little harder, because they will have opportunities to ask questions to which you didn't know the answer. As we say in my house: "that's a Google question, not a 'mom' question." If you want to be the White Knight or Wonder Woman and swoop in to save them – it may not be necessary, because you were there with them in the first place so they never got as tangled up.

You also have some special challenges.

Because you spend so very much time with your kids, it's going to be even harder for you to see those small changes as they occur. Your image of them will migrate over time, of course, but it might not move as fast as they are growing. We all have a tendency to see our kids as our precious babies – heck, I still have to concentrate sometimes to remember that my ten-years-younger sister is a grown lady of nearly forty and not the thirteen-year-old she was when I left home... or the three-year-old I taught how to read.

On the other hand, we also have the opportunity to see them growing in a much more intimate way. Many homeschooling parents report closer relationships with their children, even after the homeschooling years are done. My sister goes back to visit our dad and does house maintenance – she's always amazed by her friends who visit their folks and complain that there's "nothing to do" – and she's been doing that since college.

In my personal observations, homeschooled kids are *easier to manage* and *more respectful* of their parents' values, even when they don't agree with them. This particularly stands out in the teen years and seems to be magnified the longer the kid was homeschooled before that – in other words, the kid who started at home in third grade is less of a handful than the one who started at home in seventh, after taking family and individual personality differences into account. (The ones who start at home in seventh or ninth grade may need a little settling-in time before both parents and kids realize on a subconscious level that Things Are Different Now. In the 'trade' we call this period 'de-schooling' and we discussed this fairly thoroughly in Chapter Two.)

A big part of this is because our homeschooled kids are around us enough – and getting Quantity Time, rather than just Quality Time. Trust takes time to build between individuals, and time is exactly what we give them. They can see us as friends and confidantes.

Of course we all know to be careful about letting that go the other way. Our kids shouldn't hear about the details of our sex lives or marital issues... without leaving them so much in the dark (or trying to do so) that they're blindsided when parental Issues become family Issues. My mom – who was public-schooled – was an oversharer because she wished she'd known that her parents were miserable (they never divorced). I've tried to find a more comfortable place in talking to my kids – but yeah, they're some of my best friends.

Which *(wince, groan)* actually becomes a second piece of the problem. There's quite a number of studies that show that you become more like the five to eight people you spend the most time with. This is what results in your S.O. getting home from work and you either treating them *like* one of the kids or yourself *behaving* like a kid. When most of your time is spent with small, somewhat unreasonable people...

There're also some benefits to that, of course: kids can help you re-find your sense of play, encourage you to become more fit because you're trying to keep up with them, and teens in particular can help you rediscover a sense of idealism. There's a reason why there are so many activist mom/parent groups from MADD to PFLAG and so on.

Finding a balance is what it's all about, of course. You can't raise adults while you're acting like a kid (well, at least not if it's all the time). It's also a good thing for your kids to see other models of what adulthood looks like than the one you've settled on – or fallen into.

And that means *you* getting *out* of the house and seeing other grown-ups. (And if a self-proclaimed introvert is willing to say this...)

For years this has largely meant two things for me:

- Playgroups/Co-ops/Teams (kid-based social opportunities); and
- Parent Support Groups/Moms' Nights Out (parent-based social opportunities).

Getting a Homeschooling Group Started... the cold, hard facts

IT'S NOT HARD TO GET a homeschooling group started. Simply go to wherever your homeschool community exists and post a day and time and location that work for you. Online that may be Facebook, Instagram, someone's blog, an 'official' local group's website, and offline that might be a church, a bookstore, a health-food store, a library or even a gymnastics gym. Pick a place that you will enjoy even if no one else shows up (though they probably will).

The best times of year to get a group for kids started are just *before* the start of public school in your area, about two-three weeks *after* the start of public-school, and just after the mid-year break. Those are all at the times when people are excited about the new beginnings and are excited to add something new.

The best times of year to get a group for *parents* started are four to six weeks *after* the start of the school-year or mid-year break. That's because by that point the new, exciting curriculum or class or co-op is starting to be routine and maybe feel a bit like dragging along. At that point everyone is looking for some new idea or inspiration or even just someone who understands that this is hard and can sympathize.

You will inevitably get a large number of people at the beginning of your group – and end up with a handful of core members. Keep plugging! Even if your dream is to start something really big, great oaks have to start as small saplings. When that core group of yours continues to meet and is still there and available to the people who check in occasionally, some of those others are likely to become regulars as well.

WHAT I – AND A number of our homeschooling friends – have noticed is that it takes *at least a month* of *weekly* meetings of a *couple of hours* each *in the same location* and *with the same people* for kids to be willing to play with people other than their own siblings or cousins or that neighbor they grew up knowing. That will stretch out a bit if the location changes, even if it's all the same people, or if different people show up each time to the same place. Extraverts will become comfortable a *little* faster... and extreme introverts may take a fair bit longer. And until the kids are comfortable and not clinging to you, you don't get to really know the other parents and discover whether you are compatible with *them*. (And by then your kids may have decided these are their best friends ever...)

A project that everyone works on together can help speed things up... but only if the kids are really bought in. If it's just each family or sibling-group working together, or if it's the parents who are excited and the kids are just putting up with the project, that may actually slow the process down. On the other hand, a relatively small number of extraverted *kids* can sometimes weld the rest into a cohesive group, so long as they are both extraverted and *sensitive* to the concerns of the other children.

If a month or so to test out a group seems rather a large investment of time for 'mere' socializing, think about the following:

- grown-ups are about the same – we pick and choose who we're hanging out with by what we'll be doing together, who we'll be doing it with and what we'll get out of it vs. what we have to put into it.
- kids in school sometimes seem to get along instantly – but it's usually a week or two before they figure out the new social situation each year, and that's after spending six or more hours together every weekday – in two weeks, that's at least *sixty* hours.

A month of weekly two-hour playgroup or team meetings is only 8-10 hours – much more efficient! Some things can be rushed, but time to actually get to know people... probably can't be sped up more than that.

- this may also give *you* the time to 'test-drive' the playgroup or co-op or team before your kids really *are* deeply emotionally invested. If you discover that this awesome-seeming group is going to be uncomfortable for you on a political, religious, or other level – beyond where both you and the other families are willing to push your limits and grow – then it's better to figure that out early. I'm not particularly fussy about these things (though I've had conversations with my kids at fairly early ages about not sharing their knowledge of reproduction, evolution, or comparative religions with their friends until we're sure their parents are cool with that) but we live in the American "Bible Belt" and there are some awesome-sounding groups that aren't comfortable having my non-Christian family as part of their community no matter how private we keep our opinions and beliefs. Other kinds of frictions might involve very different approaches to homeschooling (say Classical and Unschooling or Waldorf and STEM-based PBL), cultural differences, even food or other allergies. Sometimes the group you are checking out has never even thought about a particular kind of incompatibility before a new family shows up... and where it settles out could be anyone's guess.

Finding a group where everyone's (in your family) emotional needs are being met is a Gift and to be carefully cared for and nurtured. Finding a family, or a set of families, where everyone in yours has a friend or at least someone they are willing to spend time with for picnics and birthdays and minor holidays is absolutely golden... but that's true whether you homeschool or not.

Using kid-based social opportunities

IT'S ALWAYS EASIEST TO FIND and get together with other homeschooling parents who are available during the day... so long as everyone can bring their kids. The most common situations where everyone can bring their kids are playgroups, co-ops, and teams.

Playgroups

Playgroups work best when the kids are young (infants to about twelve) and are simply happy to run around playing tag or some other active game... and then boardgames or dolls or cars or dinosaurs (or whatnot) when they wear themselves out. We've had a weekly playgroup going for some seventeen years straight – or rather a series of them, and sometimes two independent groups of friends that met on different days of the week. It's a continual process to keep a playgroup going, because friends move, choose to go 'back' to school, develop other interests... but you and your kid(s) need to have those casual, relaxed social contacts continue.

Playgroups are usually fun free-for-alls where the parents can talk and share stories (read *'group problem-solve and vent a little'*) while the kids are dashing around like crazy things. Parents are interrupted regularly by kids with questions, comments, squabbles, hunger, small injuries... in other words it's just like home but with more kids... and, thankfully, more adults.

I vary from enjoying this type of situation to feeling more than a little on edge – I do better with older kids myself, tweens and up.

Playgroups are almost *never* 'drop-off' situations – except when you have to run an errand and someone is willing to watch your kids for a little bit. Friends are accommodating like that, but the general understanding is that the parents/grandparents/caregivers/ homeschool-teachers are there to socialize just as much as the kids are.

Parents seem to start hesitating to show up for playgroups when their oldest kid is somewhere between the ages of eight and twelve. The exceptions are groups where the parents are at least as focused as their kids on hanging out with friends for an hour or two (and the kids are largely independent so that they *can*) or serious Unschoolers. What a number of parents have told me is that they start feeling like they need more 'academic time' when the oldest kid starts to reach those ages. And that cuts into social time... but when that lack is felt they often end up enrolling the kid(s) in classes and activities instead of coming back to the more freeform playgroups.

Because of these shifting needs as the kids in a playgroup grow, at this point a number of *playgroups* survive by transitioning into...

Co-ops

Co-ops or 'learning co-operatives' are just what they sound like – group homeschooling. Oftentimes the co-op will focus on one topic – led by one parent – for several weeks and then switch, but other co-ops do several topics/projects per meeting with different parents leading/ teaching, and still others will hire in someone to teach regularly, or as the need arises. Co-ops *usually* do topics outside the 'core' of Math-English, but book clubs are a common addition; this seems to be because getting a group of parents together who are both socially compatible *and* all happen to agree on 'core' curriculum is surprisingly rare but everyone can enjoy a group project in art or science or a good book.

Co-ops sometimes continue on for many years, adding and losing people as interests change and evolve. Some co-ops even morph into *cottage schools* – which are small private schools where you *do* drop your kid off for several hours and possibly for several days a week. More on this in Chapter Six.

Teams

Teams are another way to get to spend time with other parents. When my oldest daughters competed on gymnastics teams, or my younger children took indoor soccer, we spent a great deal of time in lobbies and on bleachers. It's perfectly natural to talk to the other parents – mostly not-homeschoolers – while that happens and I made some great friends that way, some of whom remained in our lives for years after the team-connection disappeared. There are opportunities to be the 'team mom/dad' and make sure there are snacks and coach-gifts and team-members' birthdays are celebrated and so on... I was just as happy to let someone else handle that, but I still had fun talking to adult people at practices and events, even while I was usually chasing toddlers, nursing babies, and dealing with sibling meltdowns.

Talking to non-homeschoolers in these sorts of situations can be very affirming of your decision to homeschool. But, of course, you have to be careful not to get too 'preachy' – nor to allow yourself to feel hurt or offended if a non-homeschooler gets 'preachy' at you!

Conversely, I've been the coach, running FIRST Lego League (www.firstinspires.org) teams since my fourth child was born in 2008 (though we took a few years off in the middle). I usually run these as *not* drop-off teams, since my goal is to work with the kids, not be a babysitter, and also because I've often needed backup when I need to take a break to parent more than coach. Once the kids get into a rhythm, they often need only minor nudges to stay on track with their projects, so then there's time to socialize with the other parents even as the coach, though the other parents, I'll note, do have a great deal more time to socialize or work on their own projects.

FIRST offers teams at various levels – but *parents* are often most interested at bringing in what I call 'mid-range' kids for these sorts of things. These kids in the 9-14 age-range are usually at the perfect stage of development for these sorts of activities, but homeschooling brings together kids of a wide variety of ability and interest levels. For example, my second son has been running Dungeons & Dragons (D&D) games at one of our playgroups for quite awhile and has had participants

> **DEFINITION**
>
> **Mid-range kids: ~9-14yos. These are the ones who still want to run around, but now they also want Projects and can work semi-independently**

(including siblings) ranging from 8-20 yeears of age. One of the great joys of homeschooling is watching people of such disparate ages choose to spend time together, but there are still developmental differences.

And one of those *differences* is that kids at this mid-range age want *Projects* that fit their *interests*.

It's a good place to start getting practice in finding or creating those things, because as they get farther into the teen years they may simply opt to stay home rather than 'wasting their time' on 'mere socializing' if there isn't a Project to draw them out. It's great to have helped raise such passionate and focused young people, but it makes it much more challenging to organize group activities for the whole family. Finding a multi-age-level *Project* can be your lifesaver, since most homeschooled

> **DEFINITIONS**
>
> **These *'Educationese'* terms are for when you explain to teacher-friends what you're up to)**
>
> **PBL: Problem/Project-Based Learning is when a variety of 'subjects' are studied through a single project that involves solving various problems.**
>
> **UNIT STUDIES: focus on a single area, but bring in various 'subjects' while covering it. Often this works well for wider age-ranges, with kids learning the parts that are developmentally appropriate.**

kids don't care how old the others on the Project are so long as they are working to the best of their abilities – and they tend to be pretty understanding about varying age/ability levels. Sometimes *(ahem)* they are more understanding about that than the coaches.

Once the kids get themselves sorted out, the parent/coach is often just there to provide moral support and occasionally point out that they are heading on a tangent. Plenty of time is left to talk to other grown-ups... and older teens.

The useful 'Educationese' terms to explain to other people what you are doing are Problem- (or Project-) Based-Learning and Unit Studies. Both are defined in the box in a little more detail.

Downsides to kid-based socializing

There are several problems with using these kid-based social interactions to maintain yourself as a reasonable adult who doesn't devolve into joining in the fight over the last donut.

The first is that it's really very fragmentary. You can't hold on a very *long* conversation with another adult until your kids are old enough and independent enough that they don't need you every few minutes... and so are *theirs*. Often times this won't be very satisfying and it may even lead to feeling *more* socially frustrated.

Another problem is that it sort of limits what conversations you can have. Controversial or emotional topics are probably better saved for other circumstances unless everyone is okay with their kids hearing about how real Santa is, where babies come from, marital issues, politics, and on and on. It's hard to build deep adult friendships without wandering into some of that territory, and sometimes you just need to cry or complain without having a row of curious little ears popping in and out. (Though there've been many tears shed by parents at my playgroups and teams – when it's all you've got, you make it work. One parent may keep an eye on everyone's offspring while others help someone cope.)

And, finally if you or one of your kids is extremely introverted – or has other difficulties with getting to know new people, this may be a challenging approach. I grew up the child of 'flaming extraverts', so

I know how to play the game, but I'm happier with much less social interaction than most of my family – and I'm also not as comfortable with all the little hugs and physical touches that many groups of women exchange so easily. My children have had issues ranging from being particularly picky about what activities they were willing to engage in to being easily offended by casual joking around to having other kids be dismissive of their interests (in math, cars, dinosaurs, insects... we've been 'dissed' in a wide spectrum of interests – I say this humorously now, but there was a fair amount of heartbreak as we went).

And all of that is on top of just the usual weirdness about joining – or forming – a group out of strangers.

Using PARENT-based social opportunities

IT'S A TRUISM THAT WHATEVER is easiest to do is what we're going to do.

If it were easier to send the kids to school, most of us would be doing that, but for whatever reason this is where we're at. It might be for short-term ease (*e.g.,* getting out of a bad fit at school or coping with family life-changes) or for longer-term ease (*e.g.,* looking ahead to a greater sense of family unity and educational opportunities), but we're looking for the easy way out.

And finding other parents to gather with in the *absence* of children is far from easy.

You have to find a place to stash your kids while you do, and so does whomever you're meeting.

You have to find a mutually acceptable time and meeting location.

And often you have to be willing to commit a certain amount of money to the Cause – even if it's just for gas and an ice tea at the bookstore where you're meeting.

These things are *hard*.

They are harder still if you live far from extended family (me), if you live far from reasonable meeting locations (me again), or if you have small children (me until very recently). I get how hard these things can be. I've had to deal with babysitters (including driving them back and forth when they were too young to drive), not enough free cash (single-income families are almost always counting our pennies), and children who are very unhappy that I was going out and wouldn't be back until long after bedtime.

Luckily, I also have an awesome spouse who could look and see the differences between when I haven't had a chance to be around grown-ups in too long and when I've had a bit of social time.

Yeah, I'm lucky – but let me be clear on something.

He has *never, ever, not even once in our twenty-five-year marriage babysat the kids.*

Not once.

He has, however, made dinner (or brought it home), taken care of bedtimes, and handled everything else while I've been out. If it's not 'babysitting' when I do it, it's not 'babysitting' when he does it. (And he's the one who actually gets slightly offended by the thought that he would 'babysit' his own kids... or when people act like he's some kind of semi-divine creature for taking all the kids somewhere without me.)

We often set ourselves up to make this part of parenting – with or without the homeschooling – hard by not acknowledging that our spouse/S.O./parent/cousin/friend/neighbor can actually keep the kids alive for a few hours in our absence. Oftentimes that's 'alive and very happy' because things were *different* and that was *special*. Ice cream for dinner? They can have broccoli tomorrow. Really. (I do draw the line at videos that I know will lead to nightmares and foods that cause violent behavior or allergic reactions. But my husband knows all those things, and it's usually a five-minute conversation with a babysitter.)

Does your S.O. try to tell you that "they miss you" and "it's been all week" and they "just want to spend the evening with you and the kids"? That sounds sweet – and most of the time that's entirely reasonable and awesome. But that's also a good time to point out that the kids need some private time with your S.O. – and honestly? *You'll* be a better S.O. to them if you can get some grown-up time and not just dump the whole day's – or week's – set of kid-related frustrations on your work-weary partner. Make your trip out a little shorter if you feel it necessary, but don't skip on spending time with other people. (So saith the voice of painful experience...)

Find a babysitter you can trust... and take a couple hours off. Even in the military they don't make you stay on duty 24/7!

Parents' Nights Out *(or MOMS' Nights Out)*

So... we all know the cruel homeschooling truth that there are a lot fewer dads who do this as the primary at-home parent. I say 'cruel' because the things that dads have contributed to our co-ops and Lego team and – occasionally – our playgroups have made it clear to me that it would be awesome to get more of them involved. It's also cruel that our society makes it feel less acceptable for a lot of men.

And, finally, it's cruel because it's even harder to find social time for groups of homeschooling dads than it is for homeschooling moms. Some groups *intentionally* exclude dads (we playtested one of those... nice people and they had their reasons, but the kids and I didn't feel all that comfortable) and more that *feel* exclusive of men simply because they are founded by groups of women and a certain vibe gets set up.

I've been running "Moms' Nights" and "Parents' Nights" for a very long time, picking up as the 'hostess' from another friend who had started the group. Over time they've morphed from being advertised "for Moms" to "for Parents". Now that we have children old enough to watch each other, my husband will sometimes join us – and I try to pass the word so that other men feel more comfortable joining in. He's still usually the only guy – but it doesn't seem to put any of the women off from coming. (And I still join the occasional "Girls' Night" with friends to watch a chick-flick or whatever. I just distinguish it from "Parents Night".)

As the 'hostess' I pick the spot to meet, the day and time, and the activity (cardgames?) if there is one, usually by soliciting the opinions of those who might come, but sometimes autocratically. I always pick a location where I will be happy, even if no one else shows up (this is also my approach to scheduling playgroups). That usually means a bookstore or coffeeshop. There was a period of nearly a year where the times/days that worked for me apparently didn't work for anyone else. It wasn't terribly useful as social time with other grown-ups – though just sitting in a *space* where there are other grown-ups interacting (and where no one was there who might suddenly *need* me) helped me stay sane!

Getting other parents to come out just to hang out and have fun is hard, though very worthwhile when you can get it to work.

Towards the end of that long dry spell where I was unintentionally hanging out at the bookstore by myself, a friend of mine who had lived in several other parts of the country realized that what she'd been missing in our area was a...

Homeschool Parent Support Group

Over the course of the following several months she ended up handing it over to me. (She's the sort of person who always has several idea pots on the boil and this was just one too many right then.) I then went on to run our Louisville Area Homeschool Parent Support Group for over five years.

We met monthly (and occasionally bi-monthly) at Barnes & Noble – which made it possible to bring at least mid-range children who could entertain themselves, and offers some food options for those who were skipping dinner to make it (me, usually, since I had the hour-drive to get there). Babies were always fine and I offered my teens as "parent's helpers" in the store to keep an eye on toddlers if people had no choice but to bring them (this being intended as an adult conversation space).

I'd post (first on Yahoogroups and then later on Facebook as the community migrated) a topic for the meeting – a 'starter' topic since most of the time we'd wander off into other directions anyways. And just because I enjoyed doing it, I'd usually put together and print a little handout with either my main talking points or things I found when I did a few hours of 'doomscrolling' (aka homeschooling research). People seemed to like walking away from a 'meeting' with something in their hands. Since, by this point, I'm often the most senior homeschooler (senior might mean any or all of: oldest, most kids, kids in college, tried the most different options, etc.) at the meeting I seem to be able to do a good job of reassuring people that it will all be okay.

The only thing that brought our group's meetings to an end was Covid – Zoom didn't really fill anyone's emotional needs, though we tried weekly meetings that way for the first couple months of lockdown. We're starting back in person – the day before this book goes to 'press'.

Why am I going to put this back together?

Because *running* the Parent Support Group means that I have a chance to keep meeting new homeschoolers – both people new to homeschooling and those new to our area... and others just new to my segment of our community. Some of those new folks have ended up becoming our very close friends. Running Parent Support Group also means that I have a finger on the pulse of the homeschooling community – for example, we would have a session each year on cottage school options and another on activities available to homeschoolers and I generated these long lists – which means that I know what *my* options are for *my* kids.

And it also gives me a chance to go out once a month, have a piece of fancy quiche and a hot chocolate and a slice of chocolate cheesecake and look at books. (Being the person who hosts-and-posts the meeting means that I get to pick a time/day/place that works for *me*. Barnes and Noble, local coffeeshops, independent booksellers with space for seating, libraries, and restaurants are often more than thrilled to reserve space for a group – for just the effort of a phone call!)

Dads also seem a lot more willing to show up to a 'Parent' Support Group – and dads who are new to homeschooling seem especially willing to come and get questions answered. We often see couples show up together just as they are getting started or while they are still considering homeschooling – and researching their options and what the community looks like.

Parents in *general* seem more willing to devote some time to coming to a 'Support Group meeting' than a 'Parents/Moms Night Out.' It's just like I described above for that transition from *playgroups* to *co-ops*. We all choose what we need and seek that out. The more value we find – or think we'll find – in a given situation, the more likely we are to put the effort in to coming. (And, conversely, the less we need that value, the less likely we are to make it. Friends closer to the end of their homeschooling career have been less likely to attend, for example. And I would get some comments on my posts that the location was just too far away... from people with a fifteen-minute drive.)

Our Parent Support Groups have ranged from entirely freeform (they usually devolve in that direction anyways) to highly structured. We've done topics ranging from 'homeschooling through high school' to 'alternate approaches' to 'dealing with challenging children'. One can set up a more specific PSG as well – focusing on, say Waldorf or Charlotte Mason homeschooling or parents of teens or special needs homeschoolers. There has been a legacy of Unschooling PSGs in my area – which I have attended on and off as well.

In many ways it doesn't *matter* what the 'official focus' of the group is, so long as you feel comfortable with the people and they aren't telling you that you're doing everything wrong. The point of attending one of these things is more than just problem-solving. It's being in the presence of adults for a little while and reclaiming your adult-self.

Raising Adults

So, WHAT DOES ALL THIS have to do with raising adults?

The first thing to doing that is making sure that we manage to be adults. And that means spending enough time with other adults that we don't forget how.

The second part is to not infantilize our kids, and in many ways that's harder. There are no easy answers of "do this and that and it will all be fine." Not infantilizing our kids means letting them grow up and become the people they are meant to be. It means helping them develop their own competencies in everything from housework to social interactions to academics – and then giving them the privilege and the weight of responsibility for those things at a point just a hair past where they are comfortable... or where they are already.

It means allowing them *agency* in their own lives.

It's another balancing act, and one that is well described by Vygotsky's Zone of Proximal Development. As you can see in the graphic, this idea is usually shown like a target. It's a strange target, though. The very center is all the things that a person can already do – it's the bullseye that we hit every time. The next circle out is the things we struggle with, but can accomplish with a bit of help. And the outer circle is the things we can't do even with help.

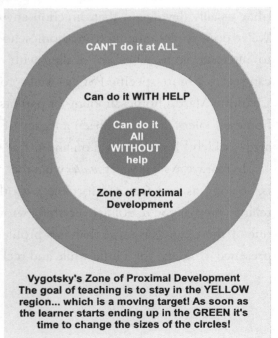

CAN'T do it at ALL

Can do it WITH HELP

Can do it All WITHOUT help

Zone of Proximal Development

Vygotsky's Zone of Proximal Development
The goal of teaching is to stay in the YELLOW region... which is a moving target! As soon as the learner starts ending up in the GREEN it's time to change the sizes of the circles!

The goal of learning is to expand the center (the green area in this graphic) by constantly staying in the middle ring (the yellow). If we are constantly trying to do things that we can only accomplish with help, we learn fastest – and we make that center 'bullseye' larger and larger. Straying into the red area – where we can't do anything useful – is discouraging, and staying always in the green area where we're already comfortable is boring and keeps us from growing.

What isn't well described is the emotional toll it takes on parents to stay 'in the zone.' It's so much easier and faster and – isn't it more *caring* to simply jump in and rescue them? And yet we know they have to do it on their own... and somehow still be there to be their safety net... without tangling them up and stopping them...

And that's where your Homeschool Parent Support Group comes in.

None of us are terribly objective when it comes to *our* kids, but it's always easy to see where other people are going 'wrong' or 'should' try something a little different.

If there isn't a Support Group in your area – or one that works for your schedule, or where you feel comfortable that the advice your getting is stuff you can choose to follow or ignore after you think about it – start your own. Find whatever online 'place' your local homeschoolers are sharing information – Facebook, Twitter, TikTok, a website, whatever – and post a day and time and place that works for you. Say you want to start a discussion on... whatever it is about homeschooling or parenting is making you pull your hair out. Or start with something where you are already comfortable and offer to share what you've learned. Find an online group if you can't get to – or get started – an in-person one (or if you prefer them that way).

There *are* homeschoolers in your area, even if you aren't sure at first where to find them (the 'secret homeschooler handshake' is to take your kids out to a public place like the library or the zoo or even a mall or big-box store and look for the other people out with kids). Pre-

Covid statistics were that between two and five percent of all school-aged children were homeschooled in the USA (not all states require reporting, hence the discrepancies). All the indications suggest that those numbers have gone up since the pandemic began.

And some of them will be your kind of people: when Bob Jones University did a study of homeschoolers in 1999, about 40% of respondents to their surveys said that one of their top reasons for homeschooling was religion. The Christian homeschoolers are certainly much easier to find since they can often organize through supportive churches. But that study tells us that 60% of homeschoolers have other things as their primary reason for homeschooling – which means there is a lot of diversity amongst homeschoolers. Even in our 'Bible Belt' area, there is a large and flourishing secular homeschooling community.

But whatever you do, find your people – even if it's not the "village" that we hear about so much raising your *children*...

It might be the "village" you need to raise *you!*

TO DO in order to RAISE ADULTS

- DO what you need to do in order to be a grown-up yourself

  - GET TIME WITH OTHER GROWN-UPS

  - Find – or found – a Homeschool Parent Support Group and meet at least monthly!

  - Get the kids into activities where there are other grown-ups for you to talk to!

  - Don't compromise on your mental health by sticking with a group where you aren't comfortable (even if the kids love it)

- Keep watch on the balance between being your kids' friend and their parent

  - No oversharing!

  - Expect that they will see you as a PERSON and not PERFECT

- Let the kids have agency, don't do everything for them

  - Keep Vygotsky's Zone of Proximal Development in mind

  - Be a safety net, not a trap

  - Teach them to do stuff that's a little beyond what they're comfortable doing... and maybe a little beyond what your are comfortable having them do.... but only a LITTLE!

Chapter Five

The Family Democracy
(and other ways to get chores done)

N OW THAT WE'VE DECIDED we're letting the kids have agency and responsibility... there's the little problem of getting them to actually *do* it. We'll talk about academics in the next chapter. For now... we're focusing on what has come to be known as 'adulting'.

This is one of the great bugaboos of most parents. We love our kids, but we hate feeling like raging monsters and lunatics when we make them do their chores. It's so much more *peaceful* when we do it for them. And it actually gets *done*.

I appreciate this one particularly right now. Because our house is tiny, we turned a mini-barn into a cottage for them and gave them a great deal of autonomy on how to keep their space. Too *much* autonomy, it turns out. They're both in college and we're trying to spread out the younger children... while still planning to preserve some space for them at home. I just went out with my overwhelmed and frustrated fourteen-year-old, who is moving out there and had been trying to clear enough space to do so. I say *trying* because clearly my daughters have inherited my hoarding tendencies... eep! We've got a long haul ahead of us... because I went for peace instead of getting on their cases.

It's always easier for the parent to go ahead and do it themselves.

Easier... but not always *better* for parent *or* child. As I've mentioned before, my kids are growing up into competent individuals (one of whom even cleans his space and gets the others to do the same...). They can cook and clean (whether or not they choose to). They know how to pay bills and sort paperwork. They are sympathetic when I'm having a tough day and will sit and comfort me or bring me a cup of tea... and they are learning to ask for help when the task is too big for them alone.

That last one is really worth all the rest and all the fuss combined. Asking for help – and then asking *again* for help when it wasn't enough or wasn't what was needed or the first person was too busy – is one of the hardest things we do as grown-ups. And, as a result, it's one of the things we don't do *enough* of as grown-ups.

The beginning of parenting involves doing a ton of extra chores – diapers and feedings and more. The end part really needs to end with the kids able to do pretty much everything any parent can do.

The middle involves getting from the beginning to the end, hopefully without the parents turning into raging lunatics or giving up and doing it all themselves.

One of the things that doesn't completely change when you start homeschooling: we all have to find a way to get basic cooking, cleaning, shopping, and home/car maintenance accomplished to a reasonable standard and in a reasonable time-frame.

Or *does* it change?

Kids (and parents) who are home all day tend to snack more. This means more dirty dishes, pots and pans. Kids who are cooking leave more of a mess than you at first expect, and that's even if they are doing it with you.

Mealtimes may flex as well – one family of my acquaintance rotated everyone's hours to match the dad, who was on night-shift. It's an option, but it means that daylight hours to get errands run and tasks completed need careful planning. It also means that social and academic opportunities – from classes to co-ops, playgroups to park-dates, need to be managed around that unique schedule. (Other homeschooling families travel extensively or spend part of every year in one location and part in another... many of the same issues need to be solved.)

Kids (and parents) who are home all day also make more of a mess in other ways and use their house more fully. As everyone learned from Covid-19, that increases costs of heating or cooling as well as food, and results in the enhanced acquisition of craft supplies, board games, science kits, hobby materials, and... toilet paper.

These aren't necessarily problems – because you now also have an increased labor force there with you all day. Well... sort of. You have a labor force, but is it a *willing* labor force? Or even if willing, is it *skilled*?

Is it fair to ask the kids to clean up, cook, repair things, teach each other, or look after each other? Is it fair *not* to ask them to do those things and leave them as passengers in their own lives? Should they be remunerated for their efforts in some way, or just expected to participate in these activities because they are part of a community?

Every family has to face these questions in their own way. But as I discussed in Chapter Four, I'm a great proponent of raising adults, not babying kids. It's good for them to learn that they have agency in their own lives – and it's good for me to see them as capable people who should be treated as such.

In this chapter we're going to look at a variety of methods for distributing chores and also helping people learn how to do things to a family-standard. We're also going to talk a bit about incentive systems and how to make getting help less work than doing it all yourself.

Should kids even have chores? And should we pay them?

I'm going to give a qualified 'yes' to the first question and a firm 'sometimes' to the second one.

Two books that have influenced my thinking on this are *Children Who Do Too Little* by Patricia Sprinkle (the author agrees it's a terrible title), and *Kids Are Worth It!* by Barbara Coloroso.

The first book was sent me by my mother-in-law when I asked for her advice on the topic – I thought that having raised five of her own, she'd have all the answers. Patricia Sprinkle has a number of useful things to say, but I refer back to her charts of 'what chores are developmentally appropriate' more than to any other part. She developed these charts by interviewing lots and lots of parents and they've made sense to me with my six – obviously you'll need to adapt these charts to your kid(s), but they're a starting point.

It's terribly important to suit the job to the child – or adult. If you have a kid who absolutely cannot stand touching dirty things *or* wearing gloves, giving them the job of washing dishes is cruel to both the kid and to everyone else who has to be present for the ensuing battles... or end up washing the dishes when it wasn't their job. It's cruel to you-the-parent as well, since it makes you turn into a monster. I've fought this battle myself – and it's not pretty. A gateway chore can be emptying the dishwasher, or putting the air-dried dishes away. They aren't dirty and icky.

Why even bother getting this touch/texture-sensitive kid to do this chore? First, because we all have to do *some* things that repel us (my kids get to hear about the *thousands* and *thousands* of dirty diapers I had to change when they complain about their chores being too icky). Second, because the family needs clean dishes put away *now*... and while there's an older brother who handles the dishwasher and another who handles the handwashables, eventually that older child is going to be gone and I'm still going to need help. (I will add that this particularly squeamish child has been offered to trade for other jobs and refuses them all – regardless of ickiness or lack thereof.)

The second book *(Kids Are Worth It!)* was originally lent me by a friend and stuck with me for its title (sometimes I just need to be able to look at the shelf and see it there as a reminder that this is true!) and because Barbara Coloroso points out that we parents are 'remunerated' for doing chores. We get to buy a book or go to a coffeehouse or pay a babysitter. We may not think of it as getting paid for chores, but it really is in a sense. She also believes that since we don't link our 'remuneration' directly to our housework that it isn't fair to do that for our kids – she thinks kids should have some of the family 'profits' simply because they are members of the family.

I agree and disagree with Coloroso on this. Money can be a useful incentive, and sometimes it's helpful to get the kids moving. Also, if they really are just sitting around and, well, breathing and playing video games, I'm not sure I agree that they are contributing enough to make it worth me paying them. It's arguable that their work is play (as Maria Montessori put it) and certainly my husband enjoys his paying work and his online chess games, as I do my writing and reading novels, but... paying kids to do schoolwork is another whole discussion and outside of the direct purview of chores.

If we're willing to consider money as just one possible incentive, then we open ourselves up to a whole set of possibilities and possible complications. But let's all face it – we bribe our kids one way or another. It might be with a hug, a story, a willingness to drive a slightly different route to see a particular statue or under a particular bridge that the family has designated 'the secret passageway', or a million other things. It's not really *bribery* – it's being *nice*. It's treating them as a person with wants, and respecting that we can fill those wants when it's reasonable.

It's treating them the way we would like to be treated.

I don't make my sick child a cup of tea because I want him to do the same for me when I'm sick – I do it because I love him and want to be nice to him. His brothers and sisters take over his chores with little argument for the same reason. It's reassuring to know we'll get similar kindnesses when we're sick, of course, but that's not the reason we initiate such actions. The reason we initiate an action, like making a sick family member a cup of tea – or doing their chores, perhaps even without being asked – is *love*... and by doing so we're building the sense within the family that we take care of each other.

Money doesn't have to be some sort of crass payment and a hold over someone's head – at least not within a family. It can simply be an honest bit of gratitude that lets the person who receives it pick their own most-appropriate treat.

I've gone through phases where the kids were paid by the chore, and others where they were paid by the week (I've done a dollar per year of age, figuring that the older ones are being more helpful). I've also gone through phases where I don't pay anything out – and the chores still get done at about the same frequency.

So why pay them at all?

Putting money into our kids' hands has been a teaching tool from the start.

When they are paid by the chore it's usually in change – every few weeks or month we sit down and 'work up' the smaller coins into progressively larger denominations. I – or one of the other kids – plays 'banker' and exchanges the smaller denominations for ones of equal value. I keep a $100 bill around so that we can compare all the way up from pennies... and my kids have known their decimals very, very well indeed.

It's also a teaching tool regarding delayed gratification. If they see something in a store and are begging me to buy it, their choice often changes suddenly and dramatically when I remind them that they can purchase it with their own money (usually by paying me back later). If they look ambivalent, I up the ante and offer to 'go halves' with them – not to torment them, but to make them think about it harder. If they really want something, they should be willing to put down what they had to work for... just like I do. (And of course, some of the things that they decide not to buy for themselves end up as birthday or holiday presents.)

When my mother-in-law sent them Barnes&Noble giftcards last Christmas, my eight-year-old and ten-year-old spent close to two hours (while the older kids and I chatted with friends) carefully making their purchases (toys, not books, LOL). They managed to choose a larger number of toys than I would have guessed, and carefully ensured they were within their limits. We used the giftcards all together, and I handed them the receipt to calculate how much they each should have had left after taxes were added – and then I gave them that back in cash at home.

We also make an irregular habit of donating money to charity. (Irregular because I'm not super at consistency.) We started out with the concept of Moon Jars (www.moonjar.com) – though we made our own out of cardboard and pickle jars. The idea here is that the jar is divided into three parts – long-term savings, short-term savings, and charity. My kids could choose how much went into each division and what the 'long-term' and 'short-term' savings were for.

Our favorite charity has so far been Heifer International (www. heifer.org) – and the kids have given several hundred dollars among them, mostly saved up from those nickels, dimes, and quarters! My oldest daughter – when she 'moved out' of our cottage to make room for her brother – left a sizable amount for us to donate. (I'm thinking she might have to agree to repurpose the money and pay her brother for all the work he's doing.)

They have also been very good about not touching their long-term savings – and adding to it. My sixteen-year-old bought himself a beater car to work on, and the older girls are using some of that money for college... along with their earnings as gymnastics coaches.

Money gives kids a greater sense of agency... just as it does adults.

However, money isn't always the best incentive.

My oldest earned over $300 the first year in change – and then she'd apparently reached her goal and was done. Money didn't motivate her any longer – and it's never been as effective with any of my other kids, even over a much shorter span of time. An offer of ice cream or to make cupcakes or a promised treat of going someplace special has sometimes been more effective with the other kids – and with the oldest child after she hit that goal. The threat/promise of friends or extended family arriving shortly has even been a bigger motivator for my kids than money!

The incentive should fit the child – and the family budget. If the parents are pinching pennies, there's no reason to pay the kids. Kids are well aware that doesn't make sense and will often feel guilty rather than pleased with such a situation. One good friend agreed to take her children to the Newport Aquarium – a favorite destination for them – if they were willing to pay for the somewhat pricey tickets (gift-money from grandparents in this case) because it's a very long drive and the family budget was tight; my friend's contribution was the cost of the gas and the not-inconsequential time she would spend driving back and forth.

The only thing I strongly suggest *not* doing in choosing your incentives is paying the kids just to 'borrow' it back again. My mom did this with me until I finally never really took seriously any cash she put in my hands as being mine to hold onto – it was always for a good reason that she needed it back, but... I'd have been happier if she didn't do the back-and-forth thing. In the end I had nothing to complain about because my parents helped pay for a lot of my college education, so I'm not bitter or bothered... just trying to find a way forward that makes more sense with my own kids.

Serious family financial issues are a different story. If your family is struggling such that your seventeen-year-old's summer job is helping keep a roof over everyone's heads – that's something you need to work out with them and make sure everyone knows the limits. The family-as-a-team concept is helpful here... but we have to be careful that we're still keeping the finish-line in mind: that kid is going to be an independent adult and we want them to be excited at spending time with us rather than wincing when they hear our ring-tone.

Or, and possibly worse, feeling like they can boss us around as we become older and more feeble. Those days will come, too... and they'll give us as much respect as we gave them when they were helpless.

Use money and other incentives carefully. Like any other tool, they can be good or bad.

So how exactly do we get the kids excited to do chores?

Well, *excited* may be a longshot, unless they are getting something really awesome out of it – which means at best, that's occasional, not on a regular basis. My fourteen-year-old is excited to have that cottage more or less to himself, but clearing out his sisters' stuff? Not so much. (On the other hand, it's making doing the dinner dishes much less awful by contrast.) And, of course, everyone has bad days where any chore seems horrid.

So, you're not shooting for them to be *excited* to do chores. You're shooting for them to get the chores done with as little whining and refusal and dawdling (which is refusal by another name) as possible.

The first thing to do is make sure the chores you are asking them to do are developmentally appropriate. Patricia Sprinkle's book is a good start at figuring out what your kids are likely to be able to do, but you will have to look at your own kids' abilities and maturity.

You also have to teach the kids *how* to do what you want and put together a set of standards that will work for everyone. Families pursuing Waldorf education have three-year-old use sharp knives to cut easy veggies for dinner – under close supervision – so that by the time they are eight they are old hands and can cut anything safely; my brother-in-law was anxious about his six- and seven-year-olds using *plastic* knives to spread peanut butter because they hadn't been through that earlier training.

If bed-making is your thing (it's not mine, so I can discuss this in the abstract), a very small child may be able to tug sheets and comforters into place but need help with changing them. And there may still be lumps and ripples.

You can point them out and let the child fix them... or let them go. But you *cannot* redo their work unless it's a matter of someone getting hurt or something getting damaged. If you redo their work (or are overly critical of the results their developmentally appropriate attempts) they will see their own efforts as useless... and then you'll end up doing it all and feeling frustrated and resentful.

And, conversely, you can't be too *un*critical. If you know that they can do a better job – say your fourteen-year-old with no known vision impairments keeps putting away dishes from the dishwasher that have chunks of food still stuck on them – then you need to gently tell them that. First of all because that child isn't ever going to do a better job if they don't know it's a problem, and second because it lets the kid know that you are still paying attention.

Obviously you'll go over the floor yourself after a glass shatters – just to check – until you've seen that they are meticulous at finding glass shards. When I realized I wasn't doing that anymore I was utterly shocked.

But silverware in the wrong places isn't life-or-death... and the linen closet looking like things got shoved in instead of folded and placed isn't either. (These *are* two of my bugaboos.)

It's perfectly reasonable to have a polite discussion where you request changes in the future. Things such as chopping the tomatoes a little finer in the *pico de gallo* or cleaning the cast iron frying pan right away instead of after food has dried onto it overnight are things the child should probably know you want changed. And if you don't tell them, they'll never know.

Chores are a way to help the child acquire all the skills they will need to live independently... someday. It's a process that can – and should – begin with helping alongside a parent and continue on over the course of days or years – depending on the task – to being capable of handling it all alone... even if you still do it together because it's more fun that way.

My kids are very capable, but they all much prefer to work when we're all doing it happily together. The nine-year-old may moan and groan about stopping her Minecraft game, but she'll go outside to help clear fallen sticks from the driveway with her brothers and sisters after a windstorm. The sixteen-year-old who rarely emerges from his room is a beacon of peace and calm – while I'm losing it – when we're preparing to receive visitors. And the thirteen-year-old who objects vociferously to cleaning his room will happily go mow our goat pasture while the others are working on other outdoor projects.

It's more than a sense of 'if I have to work, so should everyone else'. It's a sense of camaraderie.

(And it works better with my husband or older kids leading the group project, who tend to stress out less than I do.)

There's also the issue that it takes longer to teach the kids to do a task rather than just get it done yourself. And not just time – there's also less whining (well, I might be the one doing the whining, but I have control over that – at least theoretically). Of course, that's short-term thinking.

The first few times any of us do a task are a learning experience – that's true of me with a new recipe, my husband with a new power tool, or a kid with just about anything we grown-ups do by second-nature. The first few times it's going to take you longer to sweep the floor, wash the dishes, weed the garden, or re-stain the deck *with* your kid than to do it alone. Sometimes much longer. There will be mistakes and accidents. Things may need extra repairs and some things may be a lost cause.

But eventually it's well worth it.

When I was pregnant with my last child, I was so incredibly anemic that simply getting up to walk twenty feet to the bathroom was beyond me. I would sit on the sofa crying for *hours* because I needed to go so badly and... *couldn't*. I resolved the anemia, but it took a few months that also included my dad having a heart attack and recovering from triple bypass surgery with us and then a brand-new baby.

All those times when everything took extra time came back to me in spades.

My kids were able to cook, do laundry, help the younger ones keep up with school, and keep the house at a livable level of clean. I was so incredibly grateful to them – and to my husband who had always kept encouraging me not to just give up and do it myself because it was faster and easier. We did eat a lot of fast food – that my husband brought home on his way back from work – and we didn't worry about the finer points of cleaning until I was able to cope. It was crisis mode, but we survived it as a family and became stronger, more capable, and more kind to each other and to others as a result. And hopefully kinder to themselves as well – hopefully they learned that it's okay to take the time to take care of yourself and to let others take care of you. (Don't get me wrong, there were still knock-down-drag-out battles. They're kids after all – and like I said, I get *impassioned* over some things.)

Now, nine years later, I'm dealing with some long-covid issues. I'm on our weekly cooking rotation, but if I have nothing left by the end of the day, one of the kids will pick up the dinner I was planning and make it for me. Or something else if we have the supplies and they'd rather. I focus on helping them stay on-track academically and handle the scheduling and groceries – and my older teens do the driving. We're a team and we have weekly strategy meetings to make it all work out.

Finding the Family Balance and working as a Team.

So how did we get to this magickal place of perfect harmony (not) and cooperation (also not)?

We've tried several different methods over the years, which I'll detail below. There're tons of other ways to get kids to do chores of course, but these are the ones we've had the most success with for our mixed group of introverts, extraverts, neat nuts, and slobs-by-preference. None of us particularly love chores, but most of us like the results of the chores. The goal for us is to get everyone involved in taking care of the family so that everyone has a sense of competency and agency – and has the opportunity to show their love by taking care of the things they can... with respect for ages and abilities and as little whining and as few battles as possible.

The methods that have worked for us include:

1. **The Family Democracy – the most effective, at least for our large, argumentative family, but the hardest to believe.**
2. **Cash handouts**
3. **Chore charts with immediate gratification**
4. **The Race**
5. **The Leaderboard**
6. **The Bean Counter**
7. **Guilt and Begging**

In my experience, no one technique can be used for more than two to three months straight without becoming ineffective – with the exception of the Family Democracy, which we've now used for over two-and-a-half years straight, possibly because it's the most modifiable. I've rotated through the others, coming back to the ones we all enjoyed the most or that were most effective, but with any of those we still always ended up in #7 before instituting the Democracy.

Take a look and see what makes sense to you!

Option #1: The Family Democracy – the most effective, at least for our large, argumentative family, but the hardest to believe.

IN 2019 I BECAME ENTRANCED with the idea of Sudbury Schools (www.sudburyvalley.org/theory).

These 'institutions' were invented in 1968 by Daniel Greenberg, an up-and-coming young Physics professor at Columbia University, and a group of other interested parents in Framingham, Massachusetts. The idea behind the Sudbury Valley School was to treat kids like people – it's run as a democracy, with even the youngest child voting. The kids outnumber and therefore easily outvote the adults. 'Faculty' are hired on by approval of the students and their contracts must be renewed by a vote. The students even control the budget.

I began to wonder if such a system could work in a family.

I spent months talking it up around the house. I read excerpts of my sources to the kids (and my more skeptical husband). I brought up the game Nomic – a game consisting entirely of rules that are voted on. (Here are the starter rules for Nomic: http://www.gamecabinet. com/rules/Nomic.html Here are the 'fun' rules for a version I hosted online for some friends back in 1995... this is a mirror site, not my own: https://www.nomic.net/deadgames/misty/ NomicUpdate.html).

My children – especially the oldest two, who had already spent several years participating in model government programs – were excited.

On January first of 2020, we began.

It hasn't been smooth sailing – and no, we haven't given over control of the family finances. Nor does my husband usually participate, unless we need to break a tie. We do a Family Meeting almost every Sunday – and the first two weeks the meetings lasted close to eight hours each as the kids hammered out all the procedural stuff and rules. I should say 'the kids and I' since I was definitely there and a part of it, but my older daughters were much more familiar with parliamentary procedure and judicial procedure after all the model government team stuff they'd been doing for several years.

We elect four officers each week: a Chair to run the following week's meeting; an Executive to remind people to do their chores; a Judge to resolve conflicts; and a Deputy Judge (now known as the DJ and given the option to play music all week) in case the Judge is involved in an altercation. Naturally my younger sons – then eleven and nine – who were the first elected Judge and Deputy Judge got into a fight with *each other* that first week. (The case was sent to Jury – the next Family Meeting – and resolved.)

We pass 'laws' – under the numbering system from Nomic, with our '100-level' laws being the most important and hardest to change, beginning with our Law 101: Be Nice (arguably everything else is just an elaboration of that... but the devil is in the details, so those elaborations are necessary). We pass amendments. Bills must be written up in advance and posted for public commentary. Lawsuits must be properly filed, with the appropriate laws referenced and judicial precedent is consulted in the decisions. We've had several hundred Lawsuits and something under a hundred Bills – most Bills actually fail when subjected to the intense scrutiny of seven or eight very interested people.

Our very first Law was actually a Bedtime Law... *requested* by the three younger children (the older ones had graduated out of needing bedtimes by then). They actually picked somewhat *earlier* hours than their father or I would have suggested!

So, what is the result of all this craziness?

First off, the *kids* have passed Laws requiring them to finish whatever schoolwork the parents assign each day before any screentime is used. Our assignments are pretty short – again, we go all year and all week, taking breaks when we go on vacations, aren't feeling great, have Big Events to plan or execute, and so on. At this point, my eleven-year-old is handing me his completed work as soon as I crawl out of bed, and my nine-year-old is cutting back on her screentime (one of my personal goals is to help them learn to set reasonable limits on screentime for themselves) when she doesn't feel like doing her work. My thirteen-year-old often rises even later than me, but he also gets his work done without complaint, and the same with the sixteen-year-old.

There's no more bargaining to get their way instead of sticking to established rules, and rarely any fighting. If there are complaints it's because we had a misunderstanding about what was expected – and those misunderstandings do sometimes get loud and raucous, but they're usually not all that unreasonable. We're working on frustration tolerance also, and if someone takes a few minutes to cool off (that's what we're going to call storming off while declaring they will never do math again) and then comes back with a calmer disposition to discuss the problem... that's growth. The idea is that they'll have these behaviors sorted out by the time they graduate; it's just nicer for *me* if they figure it out earlier. (And, yes, occasionally I mutter dark thoughts to myself about how peer pressure in school would help eliminate the storming off... but then I think about all the bad words and drugs and bullies I don't have to worry about... I'm probably coming out ahead still.)

The second obvious result is that the house is *not* any neater or cleaner than it was before we started this Grand Experiment. It's not really any dirtier, though, so I can't really object.

The third result – which is only obvious if you knew us before and after and are here much of the day (meaning no one else sees this, not even my husband, really) – is that there is a lot less *fighting and yelling*. Mostly a lot less of *me* fighting and yelling.

This is certainly at least in part because the kids have gotten older – but while some of them have gone into less combative phases of life, others have followed them into the phases they just exited. Overall, I'd guess we have about the same level of grumpy kids as before.

But we elect an Executive each week: it's *their* job to handle reminders and it's *not mine*. This person hasn't had weeks and months and *years* of having to nag people. To them it's just a week. And next week someone else can do it, or they can run for re-election. (This is still the least popular position – though it's mostly because it requires more regular work than the other three positions. Everyone wants to be Judge because the cases have dropped off drastically in recent months.)

I do still end up being involved in the reminder process. However, the process is now that I tell the Executive, and the Executive tells the person who hasn't done their chore. They get three documented reminders, after which the Executive can file a Lawsuit if they still haven't done their chore. (Anyone can sue over an incomplete chore that infringes on their ability to complete their own chore or other task or need.)

Occasionally I grumble and grouch (when the Executive hasn't been on the ball) and the kids have to remind me to follow due process.

Occasionally I take over and make people do things when I haven't been elected. It usually gets me sued. If the situation isn't deemed to have been urgent enough to have invoked the Emergency Powers Law that temporarily returns all 'normal' parental powers to me or my husband, then we are given a consequence. We've both had to write lines (think "I will not yell when asking is all I need to do" ten times), do an extra chore, or apologize. A few times I've been assigned to do (easy) push-ups under our Immediate Consequences Law that was put in place to break up and distract from altercations as well as to prevent legal delays from disconnecting infraction from result for (especially, but not only) the younger kids. It's always done very fairly and thoughtfully, with a Judgment written up that can be appealed.

The kids have to agree on allocation of chores – and if someone wants to give up a chore everyone agrees is necessary, they have to negotiate to trade with someone else. Sometimes, when it becomes clear that one person has volunteered themselves into too much work, the group has worked to even out the load a bit – they even did that for me once, acknowledging that some chores, such as scheduling really had to be left in my hands and giving me credit for that. When my second daughter headed off to college, re-allocating her chores – even though she had some heftier ones as the eldest child living at home – it took all of five minutes to arrive at a distribution that made everyone happy.

Note that this system can work with any of the other chore-incentive methods that follows... but it doesn't have to. The kids have so much agency – so much power, to put it bluntly – over their lives that it's not about a top-down government (parents) imposing incomprehensible rules on everyone else. Certain chores have been written into 'law' so that the standard is clear – but the kids mostly wrote, or at least altered, those laws. For example, each pair of roommates (including myself and my husband) are required to have a Roommate Agreement – there is a basic minimum standard that includes health and safety, and they can default to that. Every week an agenda item for the meeting is a check-in with each pair of roommates as to whether their Agreement needs to be modified and whether it is being upheld. It's a safe and calm space to bring up recurring issues. I don't have to pay them money or reward them with treats to get things to work.

Does this sound a little insane? Like, say, the inmates are running the asylum? (Leaving aside that neither home nor school should be a prison camp.)

It's been well over two-and-a-half years now and this system is still in place. We had a 'constitutional convention' a few months ago to streamline our body of Laws, but no one has seriously suggested getting rid of the Family Democracy, not even my husband.

Nothing else has lasted us this well.

'Nuff said.

Option #2: Cash handouts

THIS IS JUST WHAT IT sounds like. Every now and then I realize that I really meant to setup some formal method of compensating my kids for all the stuff they do – and that I haven't given them anything for a while. Since my kids are such savers, it's really me shooting myself in the foot, because money in their Moon/pickle jars (or bank accounts) is money that's being set aside for big later expenses. (This is more true of the older three...)

When I reach this point, I usually just give them some amount of money. This is closer to the dollar-per-week per year of age I mentioned earlier, though at this point I'm a little less about connecting age to payments. My sixteen-year-old is actually at least as helpful as my eighteen-year-old, so it would be silly to pay him less just because he's younger. The younger ones get somewhat less, based more on how much they do for the family than by their age. I also don't pay for whining, so a cheerful attitude (or at least a quiet one) gets a better payout.

I try to stick to this... but I'm terrible at consistency, so it lasts a few weeks or a month.

I also do the occasional cash payout for particular chores. Cleaning the kitchen is my responsibility to get done – but if one of them is willing to take $5 for it and I'm tired, we're both happy.

I've suggested they negotiate for higher payments if it's not enticing enough – both because I want to get the job done and because I want them to be confident enough to ask for a raise when they are adults. Sometimes they ask an outrageous amount and I decline – sometimes we reach a happy middle. With six kids, there is also the possibility of a brother or sister being willing to take my somewhat higher second offer while the original negotiator holds out for their preferred payment – no unions here (so far)!

Cash payments tend to work better when I offer them while showing a hint of my guilt for not having kept up with things. "This is

117

to thank you for all your hard work," makes it sound more like gratitude and an honorarium rather than a 'job' to which they can say 'no'. And having received money for work already done tends to make my kids feel happy with me – or slightly guilty themselves so that they feel they need to do a bit more to *really* earn what's already in their hands.

I actually like this method fairly well. If you've studied animal training (I highly recommend *What Shamu Taught Me About Life, Love & Marriage* by Amy Sutherland) you'll already know that irregular reinforcement is the most effective way to maintain a behavior once it's established. So, once they know I will pay them and for what, this is very effective at making all of us happy and the house cleaner.

Option #3: Chore charts with immediate gratification

THERE ARE SEVERAL PROBLEMS WITH standard chore charts.

The first is that crossing something off or checking a box isn't all that satisfying for some of us. Some parents use star stickers or other such point systems instead, but that takes some of the agency out of the child's hands.... and therefore, some of the responsibility that these charts are supposed to help build out of the equation.

A second is that if there is a greater reward after finishing the chart, what do you-the-parent do when the daily chore was only accomplished four days out of the week? Or two? Or *one?* Do you pay equally for all the stars or checkmarks? Or, conversely, if you are paying by-the-job for at least some jobs, how do you handle the kid who realizes – as my sister did at about age seven – that they can wash the *same windows* over and over and over again and get paid each time?

A third is that there is a lot of upkeep, beginning with having to produce a new one regularly, keep stickers in store, etc. My mom 'solved' this one by making me a chart on fine graph paper that was supposed to last for the whole month. Needless to say, I didn't actually keep it up for more than the first week and she forgot about it around the same time (lack of consistency in these matters is apparently hereditary...).

118

So the awful thing hung on the wall just making us both feel guilty until she would take it down.

Obviously nowadays we can just print or copy off a new chore chart as often as we want, but there's other kinds of upkeep: the parent still needs to remind the kid to look at the chart, to cross off the chart, and to continue providing stars or whatever finish-point rewards. A chart that is supposed to earn a kid a big payoff and then gets forgotten by both parties generates nothing but disappointment and is going to make it harder for the next attempt to be successful.

My mother's other parent-time-and-labor-saving idea was to put *everything* on the one chart. Why make a chart to remind me to brush my teeth and a chart to remind me to feed the cats when one chart would do? Why offer verbal reminders when the whole point of the chart is to prevent arguing about what is and isn't the kid's to do? This, however, resulted in everything in micro-writing and that – coupled with my mother's tendency to take back any money she paid me – made me even less enthusiastic about the chart.

So, having come from all these negative chart experiences, I was hesitant about using one until I read Sutherland's book and was introduced into the world of animal training. The key was to get as close to instant reward for an improved behavior as possible.

For me the resulting solution was to:

1. keep the number of items on the chart few so they were each noticeable

2. keep the chart to one week at a time

3. assign a monetary value based on how valuable the chore is to *me* – so emptying the dishwasher might be a quarter, but a personal hygiene item should be a penny since it's more of a reminder than something for others. All values had to be change I had on hand and no more than one coin per job

4. the coins had to be physically attached to the chart so the child could remove them as soon as the task was completed, giving them the agency and power

Minor modifications involved setting certain chores that had to be accomplished in a specific timeframe to take the coin – such as feeding the dog or emptying the dishwasher.

The charts themselves are either handmade or printed. I slide them into a clear plastic page-protector, along with a piece of cardstock or cardboard for stiffness. The whole thing is attached to a wall with thumbtacks – ideally a wall where both I and the kid will see it regularly throughout the day. The money is usually attached coin by coin with small pieces of transparent tape (though for a while I used transparent tape to create little pockets instead).

This is the method by which my eldest child earned over $300 in one year.

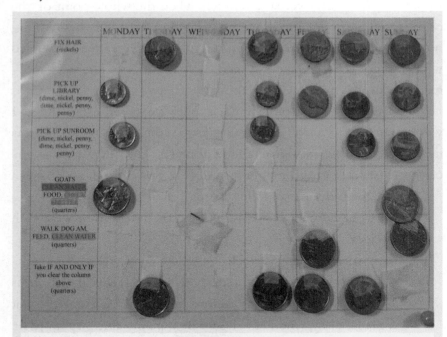

COIN CHART

Note that the coins are only attached with a tiny piece of tape so they can be easily removed. The chart is inside a plastic page protector, so I can change it out easily and the tape comes off easily. We actually re-use the tape! The coin notations were for my oldest son – whom I started paying to refill the chart since it wasn't my favorite job!

It worked quite well when we had a wall right in our kitchen/dining area so that it was easy to see the charts. It works less well in our current home due to architecture.

It also works less well than the previous two methods (cash payouts and the Family Democracy) for kids who really aren't all that money-driven... which includes most of my younger kids. They *like* the idea, but they forget to take the coin off the chart when they do their chore.

It's also a fair amount of upkeep, having to attach all those coins every week. In its latest incarnation, I ended up paying my sixteen-year-old to repopulate the charts for his younger siblings.

On the other hand, it allows you to specify different values for different tasks accomplished – or to alter the payout if you're trying to build a new habit. And if you want a particular task done every other day, you simply only put coins up for those days.

It also makes it very clear what the reward is. I did try adding an extra coin at the bottom of each column which could be claimed if the day was emptied, and a quarter for the week for each row. For example, if the dog was fed and walked each morning, an extra quarter. This didn't seem to help my kids remember to either collect their money or do their chores (though the dog always got walked and fed).

It's worth a try – if you have a kid who goes for this, you're golden.

Option #4: The Race

DID I MENTION THAT MY kids are competitive? After talking to a friend who was really into 'Gameschooling' I decided to try gamifying chores.

Using a piece of posterboard I created a sort of hybrid between Monopoly and the Game of Life. This is actually *still* on our refrigerator even though we haven't used it in over six months.

The key concepts in effective game-engagement seem to be: leveling up, being able to out-compete someone else, a dash of randomness, some ability to strategize, and very clear rules. (There are books about this... I made up my version after some rather casual conversations with that friend. She was developing her own system that included both schoolwork and housework. She has a degree in psychology and actually studied the whole idea of gameschooling in detail before going this route.)

I sweetened the pot by paying them real money (Pass GO and collect 200¢).

After each couple of circuits, they got to 'level up' by having their icon 'evolve' (this was a Pokémon influence). I chose a

> **DEFINITION**
> **Gameschooling: an approach that uses the prominent features of games (competition, leveling up, some randomness, and some ability to strategize) to turn academic work into a game. Educational games fall into this category as well.**

Pokémon character that had multiple evolutions. My oldest son chose to be a Corvette (8 versions available!). If my oldest daughters had participated, we'd likely have had evolving dinosaurs and various stages of insect development as options. Perhaps your kid would be excited to be able to morph their 'game avatar' into every possible version of Batman or every Green Bay Packers quarterback in sequence.

The Chance cards served to incorporate that bit of randomness – sometimes requiring them to do an extra chore or move back a few steps and sometimes accelerating their progress.

The Battle Cards were a complete flop, I'm sorry to say. The idea was that if they landed on the same space, they had to play a game and the winner got to move ahead a space. At the time, these were all simple games like Candyland – in part because the youngest child needed to be able to participate and in part because I was trying to (ahem) *subtly encourage* the older kids to play age-appropriate games with her. I underestimated her abilities to play more complex games as well as the effectiveness of the bribe; they just piled their avatars on top of each other and were happy.

The Pass GO space was popular, of course, but the Jail/GO-to-Jail pair didn't add much from anyone's perspective.

And the evolutions and acceleration of movement with each evolution quickly got out of hand with my oldest child who was participating: that Corvette was whizzing around the board in a day or two (he used up all 8 generations of Corvettes and moved on to Camaros). I didn't mind rewarding him for his efforts, since this child is my only enthusiastic chore-doer, but it made the younger three give up since there was no way to keep up with him and the situation was only magnified with each round.

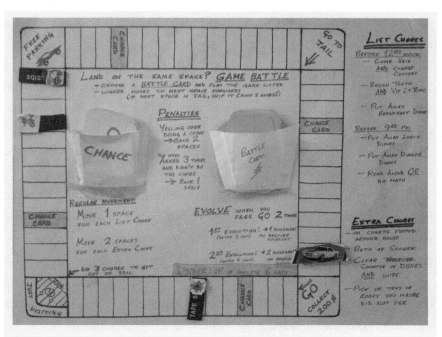

THE RACE
(as my kids christened this attempt to 'gamify' chores).
Note the Corvette and the various Pokémon characters.
I felt like the rules should be simple enough to write the whole thing on the board. I'd make a few tweaks now, but this worked really well!

Nevertheless, they had sufficiently fond memories of the thing that the younger three *asked* me to re-start it (actually, they got the family to 'pass a law' at the weekly meeting that I had to) for just the three of them. The joy didn't last quite as long this time – perhaps a month when the first round went about three months. Among other things the oldest of *them* was now far outdoing the youngest *two*.

However, the fact that they had enough fun to want to do it again – and it got a great many chores accomplished while it was in place – suggests that this is something I should tweak a bit.

Option #5: The Leaderboard

As you might guess, this was inspired by 'reality' TV – in our case, *Dancing with the Stars*.

This one actually works with any other method. It was simply a matter of keeping a set of name-cards visible and each day (or week) the person who got the most chores accomplished gets moved to the top.

In our incarnation of this approach, the person at the top of the leaderboard got to choose from the possible list of chores first, and then on down, so that there was some concrete reward for having finished in first place. I had a set of chore-cards, and we'd all get together and take turns picking, going in rounds until everything necessary had been chosen. I had the chore-cards color-coded for '*needs* to be done daily', '*needs* to be done weekly', 'would be *awfully nice* to get done this week', etc. Some chores paid better, some were inherently ickier, but the idea was that there was an advantage to getting a higher ranking.

The downfall – for us – was that my kids *hate* change. They would rather do the same chore (that they don't like) for five years straight rather than switch to one they *might* not dislike as much. So, my incentive system was off. (As an example of how averse to change my family is: my oldest son made the same dish – noodles and tuna sauce – on

Thursday night for something like four years straight. The rest of the family began using that as the way to tell what day it was... and, when the overly rich white sauce started upsetting too many tummies and we had to switch things up, the kids with the upset stomachs – who had given up eating the stuff on their own – objected to the change!)

For families where change is a pleasure, or adds some spice, the Leaderboard system – or perhaps a 'dial' where everyone's chores rotate to the next position daily or weekly – might work. The dial system is actually one I saw another family implementing happily and have always yearned to try... but since my kids hate change... oh, well. *Know thy own rugrats* is the cardinal rule.

Option #6: The Bean Counter

THIS ONE (FINALLY) IS COOPERATIVE rather than competitive. And yet my ultra-competitive kids liked this, too. They actually *really* like supporting each other... though I sometimes wonder if the ulterior motive is that they somehow see us as 'out-competing' *other* families... Sometimes it's better not to ask.

In this case you have a jar – go ahead and buy a tall, narrow, *clear* vase from a craft store. Narrow is important or it takes forever to earn a reward. You mark off levels on the jar or vase and associate a treat with each level – something for the whole family, like ice cream or a movie or a trip to a favorite playground. For a particularly big teat and a narrow enough jar, you could just have a treat for filling the whole thing.

The idea here is that every time *anyone* in the family does something that you'd like to reward – such as remembering to take out a stick of butter after using up the last one or puts their shoes away properly or helps a brother or sister with tying their shoes, anything kind or thoughtful – you drop some beans (or noodles) into the jar. (We used noodles because they take up more space, but then I had to overcomplicate it by having bigger noodles for bigger acts of kindness...) When the jar reaches one of the pre-determined levels for a treat, the whole family celebrates together.

A variation is that anyone can add beans to the jar when they see an act of kindness being done – though of course you have to feel like you can trust the kids not to play the system. The converse is that if the parent is the only one (or ones) who can add to the jar you have to be very generous in your willingness to add beans.

The Bean Counter is actually intended as a technique for improving the whole family's temper and appreciation for each other rather than getting chores done. If the kids (and parents?) have just sort of ended up tending to see – or expect – the worst of each other rather than the best, the Bean Counter can help... though it can probably be modified to include chores as well, if the doing of chores is seen as 'helping the family to exist' and as a co-operative effort. It's a sort inverse to a 'swear jar' where you ante up some cash every time you swear and then either donate the money or buy everyone else a treat.

This is a variation of the positive parenting technique called 'catching them being good'. All too often we end up catching our kids being 'bad' – or at least we end up in a situation where it feels like that's all we're doing. It feels like that to the kids as well, and they develop a feeling that either we-the-parents are unfair and don't trust them, or that they really *are* bad. It's hard to break that cycle – especially when you have objectively real behavioral Issues going on, as I know from painful personal experience. The Bean Counter jar can be a powerful tool to help you adjust your own perceptions and see that your troublesome kid (or kids) is actually 'good' more often than you think – and your acknowledgment of that helps the kid know you are seeing it.

It's also important that you never remove beans in the Bean Counter, unlike the Hogwarts House gems in the giant hourglasses from the Harry Potter series. After all, if the main point is to reward positive, kind behaviors, then you don't want to create a negative feeling around the whole thing or a sense that mistakes will be punished. Children (and adults) are still growing and will screw up occasionally. Just because my son yelled at his sister for playing with his toys without permission doesn't take away how he made sure there was enough milk for her cereal even though she was the last to the table at breakfast and he really wanted a little more. (It also doesn't mean he shouldn't apologize right now.) Kindnesses aren't wiped away by mess-ups, but taking beans out makes it look like they are.

And, as with everything else, this can be made competitive. My husband and I initially tried this (using those multicolored glass 'jewels' that are sometimes used to line fish tanks or fill decorative jars) to sort of actually replicate the giant hourglasses for the four Houses in Hogwarts. We made a variety of mistakes, beginning with using jars that were much too big, so filling them was next to impossible. And possibly we started this way too young – I think the older kids weren't more than seven and five. And lastly, we really didn't need to foster a sense of competition in being nice. (Arguably, with our kids we didn't need to foster competition at all!)

But, most critically, we were using this without specific goals and without any clear explanation of why jewels would be added. No clear goals equals no obvious results... so, like many other things, this competitive version dribbled away over time.

The mistakes we made with the Bean Counter in co-operative mode were slightly different. I overcomplicated it (different sizes of noodles). I still had too large a jar. And the treats for reaching a level turned out to be either too big for immediate rewards (*e.g.,* take everyone Go-Karting, which required planning ahead, since it's over an hour's drive away) or too plebian to really feel like a reward (it turns out we go have ice cream a little too often... even though everyone liked the idea of using that for a reward) or caused too much argument (*which* boardgame?). My seventeen-year-old says he didn't like it because there was no personal incentive to earn noodles since they were all combined – a sort of 'Tragedy of the Commons' issue writ small... and possibly another example of how competition works better for my family.

And, finally, my kids actually get along pretty well with each other without external incentives. We've had bad times, of course, but apparently telling them we're a team and we support each other sank in somewhere along the way. Rewarding desired behavior that occurs naturally can run the risk of training the behavior to be a response to some anticipated treat instead of simply acknowledging and appreciating it. Rewarding it *sporadically* usually is fine and actually helps... but the Bean Counter jar was right along that fine line for us when we tried it out, though I know of at least one family that has used it for several years successfully. The mom in that case said that they would go through spates where they would forget about it for several months and then pay attention for a few weeks (in my house it would vanish under projects and books and papers if it was that neglected...).

Our jar has been set aside for some years now, but we may come back to it.

Option #7: Guilt and Begging

OKAY, THIS MAY SOUND A little strange to include in a list of how to get your kids to grow up into the kind of adults who can and will take care of themselves and others – and their current family and home – and be helpful to *you*. None of us want our kids to grow up feeling like they are terrible people or they had overburdened childhoods. Most of us don't want them to think we are overburdened either. Or that *they* are a burden to *us*.

So, clearly, this technique is a delicate one, and I advocate using it as sparingly as possible.

Before we delve into what I mean in calling this a 'technique', let's cover a few definitions.

Many of us have very complicated relationships with the concepts of Guilt and Shame. *In this particular context* I want you to think about the terms this way:

- Guilt: means an INTERNALLY IMPOSED feeling that says you did something you shouldn't (or didn't do something you should have) and that you need to make up for it to whomever or whatever was harmed by your action or inaction. Guilt asks you to do something NOW.

- Shame: is an INTERNALLY IMPOSED feeling that says you have a behavior pattern that is causing harm to you or to others that you need to mend. Shame asks you to make LONG-TERM changes.

Note, please that none of this is about EXTERNALLY imposed feelings. It's not about someone else telling you that you are bad.

Just as important, both the parent/caregiver and the child involved in this sort of an interaction need to be confident and comfortable with each other. There has to be an assumption of love and that both people are good people who just aren't seeing quite eye to eye *in this moment.*

And lastly, that's an *internal* assumption as well. It's not just about you-the-parent knowing that your child will love you – but being able

---

DEFINITION

Guilt: means an INTERNALLY IMPOSED feeling that says you did something you shouldn't (or didn't do something you should have) and that you need to make up for it to whomever or whatever was harmed by your action or inaction. Guilt asks you to do something NOW.

DEFINITION

Shame: is an INTERNALLY IMPOSED feeling that says you have a behavior pattern that is causing harm to you or to others that you need to mend. Shame asks you to make LONG-TERM changes.

to prevent yourself from going into a guilt-spiral. Of course you need to be sure you kid won't go into a guilt-spiral either, but the best way to make sure of that is usually to model it for them.

If you aren't *absolutely sure* you can handle a bit of Guilt and Shame (as defined above) and that so can your child, avoid this technique like the Black Plague.

How to use Guilt and Begging effectively

We all use this 'technique' to some extent. It's our default when everything else has failed. And we all know what *doesn't* work: whining, repetition, irritability, resentment, yelling, sarcasm, and rudeness.

What does work? Letting your kid(s) see your honest frustration. Keeping your tone well-modulated – though if it veers off into teary or a *little* squeaky as you try to keep it calm and even can feel really honest. Actual real tears – though those have to be sparing; if you cry every time you use this it will turn into a Boy Who Cried Wolf situation and they will tune you out.

The 'trick' is to be... honest. To not be using this as a 'trick' or a 'technique' but to honestly be letting your kid(s) see that you're overwhelmed and frustrated and need their help. Everyone loves to be the White Knight and come in and save the day – occasionally. Letting the people who care about you see you as *vulnerable* every now and then... and *humble* enough to beg for help when you are so vulnerable will really speak to them.

That's the Begging.

The Guilt needs to be wielded with an even *lighter* touch. Guilt and Shame are feelings that we don't like – because they mean we have screwed up – and so they are the easiest to tune out in order to restore our sense of 'not being a bad person'. In order to use Guilt to motivate your kid(s)... you are trying to *induce* that INTERNAL feeling of needing to make things right, rather than *impose* an external feeling that just makes them feel awful.

How can you do this? It's harder to explain because every situation is different. In general, however, if you are obviously 'soldiering on' for the benefit of the family – or trying – you are setting up the situation where the kid(s) can look and see that they need to step up a bit more.

But *beware!* You *do not* want to come across as a 'martyr' or that you are sacrificing yourself for your family. Why? Because that is going to go one of three ways:

1. your family will *never notice* because you're doing such a good job of sacrificing yourself – which is bad for your family because it reduces their agency in their own life and bad for you because it puts you in a dependent position. That may seem backwards, but what happens when your kid(s) eventually *does* grow up and become self-sufficient? The self-sacrificing parents are the ones who 'empty nest' so hard that their adult children start to fear their visits; or start to think that the parent is incompetent and need to be taken care of; or who rely on their parents long past the time they should be looking after themselves and are then not capable of taking care of their own children and spouse... or you, when you're old and frail. In the worst case, the too-effective self-sacrificer can be utterly lost even with a helpful, supportive family. I saw my own mother do this – a strong, capable woman who nevertheless fell apart physically, emotionally, and mentally when my sister went to college... even though my sister was very involved with our parents (I was living a thousand miles away, but we spoke regularly by phone). It was... terribly sad.

2. The 'martyr' parent's efforts are noticed by the family, but the 'martyr' parent is assumed to be choosing this because that's what they *want* to do. (My mom fell into this category some as well.) It's easier to let someone do stuff for you... and if you get the feeling that the person who is doing everything may be complaining a lot, but secretly loves what they are doing... or if you can tell yourself that...

3. The kid(s) begin to resent the 'martyr' parent because it seems like every time they turn around they're being told they don't do enough; they don't care enough; they *are* not enough.

The key, then, is to let your family know – gently – that you are overwhelmed and need help to get back on track. Perhaps you even need help to develop a *plan* to get back on track (that's something older kids may really get interested in helping with). You have to be *genuinely grateful* for the help, even if it's not quite what you were helping, and you have to be willing to let your kid(s) do some of the problem-solving. The goal should be to use their aid to get you past a tough spot – and only when there really is no other option. A little bit of humble embarrassment that you ended up in a pickle doesn't hurt. I procrastinate terribly about filing paperwork – just copies of our bills for later reference – and sorting through mail with bills. I procrastinate and then it's huge and overwhelming and I feel sick and stupid and... we all probably have something that hits us like that. One time I actually hired someone to help me get it all put together and make the calls to the various health-services companies I was dealing with (I also hate talking on the phone). But most recently my second and third oldest kids helped me sort the papers and get back on top of things... when I asked them humbly and with a bit of panic in my voice and face. It turned into a great opportunity to show them all the sorts of bills we have to pay and discuss how family finances work.

And I'm absolutely serious about that 'developing a plan' to get back on track and avoid whatever pitfall put you in that situation. If your kid(s) see that this is *temporary*, and that there is a future that doesn't involve this particular problem, then you are teaching them valuable lessons about reaching out for help and overcoming obstacles. My kids have seen me run myself into the ground more than once. So now, as we come out of pandemic isolation and I'm looking for social opportunities for them and me again, the kids are insisting I keep activities at a reasonable level and that we have a plan to satisfy everyone's needs without making me collapse again. Kids like knowing what the path forwards is and what the ramifications are.

Begging is the tool you use to let your kid(s) know that there is something you need help with – and that you are super serious about it. This isn't something you *could* handle, it's something you really need them to do.

Guilt is what your gentle, polite, *humble* begging – following all the other ways of asking – will trigger in them. Your kid(s) INTERNAL motivation will come because they have realized you aren't sacrificing yourself for the family because you want to, but because you're desperately treading water... and they have the ability to throw you a life-preserver.

(It should go without saying that you should never, ever, ever ask your kid to throw you a life-preserver that they can't lift. A five-year-old can fetch you a book or a box of Kleenex when you're sick, but not make you a cup of tea. A seventeen-year-old might be able to drive you around when you sprain your ankle, but can't be your therapist. Get the help you need from other grown-ups, too.)

So...

When can you use Guilt and Begging then?

First, you want to use it in *very small doses*. If you have a chronic illness – and most of us have known someone with a chronic illness, even if we haven't had one ourselves – you know that people's interest in helping wanes with repeated efforts. It's 'compassion fatigue' and it hits all of us. For example, it may wrench your heart to hear your baby crying for the fifth time in the night, but you are so incredibly tired by then that you might pretend you were deeper asleep until your spouse gets up. (Yes, that was me. And him. We have six kids. There was a whole lot of tired going on... even with the first one, to be honest. Getting used to being a parent feels brutal even when you are entirely on board, it was a planned pregnancy, you have two involved parents, and your kid isn't particularly difficult. I really admire people who did it the other ways. You deserve all the chocolate the world can give you. And naps.)

Second, you want it to be for *important* things. Things that *matter* to you. And yes, that can be 'petty' things if they matter to you.

It's really stupid, but if the butter is too hard to spread on my morning toast because I had to get out a stick from the fridge when I woke up because someone used it up (or no one else noticed it was used up)... I feel unloved. It's a tiny, stupid thing, but it sets the tone for my whole day.

If there is one, tiny thing that will make your life happier, it *might* just be important enough to make a fuss about so that the people who love you and want you to be happy know that they can make that difference. If it's that small – it's an easy thing for them to do. This is why we all re-washed that *same* plate or spoon or cup or shirt for our toddlers, right? Because we loved them and giving them that one thing that made them so much happier was worth it to us.

Well, *our* happiness is worth it to *them*, too.

If what matters to you is a *big* thing, that's okay, too. Big things might include making sure the level in your gas tank isn't about to leave you needing a tow (for your teenage driver borrowing the family car) or writing those thank you notes for graduation gifts or making sure there is a 'fire lane' through your kid's room to doors and windows and bed.

And, clearly there can be several things at the same time, BUT...

Thirdly, don't use Guilt and Begging on more than *one* thing at a time. Separate your uses of this as much as possible. For small things (like a stick of butter) maybe several hours is enough. For something like the gas tank, it might be several days. And that's not just between reminders about the butter, but about the spacing between guilting your kid(s) about the butter *and* doing it over the gas tank.

Our visceral reaction to Guilt and Begging is to mix it all together, which results in nothing standing out. The kid (or spouse) will just feel a general miasma of misery focused around you. Nothing will change, you'll feel more frustrated, and the family's mood will deteriorate.

Which brings us to...

Fourthly, be *crystal clear* about what your issue is with the situation and what must be done to mend it. This is back to goals again.

And you might ask "why not just start with this 'fourthly' business? Why not just tell them exactly what the problem – and solution – are in the first place and do it without all the drama implied in the term 'Guilt and Begging'"?

My answer to that most excellent question is that *of course* that is what you should have done. This goes back to the chapter on stating your goals. Be clear, be explicit, and be detailed. Whether or not you stipulate how a problem is to be solved depends on the problem and the problem-solving skills of the other person. You wouldn't expect a five-year-old to figure out how to organize their time to make dinner (or, probably, to make a 'dinner' more complex than sandwiches), but you might expect a ten-year-old to have some ideas and want to give them a chance to see if it will work the way they think it will. And a fifteen-year-old (if they have been cooking for a while) can probably handle the entire process with only the occasional request for help or advice.

Ideally, just telling them what needs to be done would be the end of it.

But, if we all lived in an ideal world, the word 'nagging' would never have been invented.

Face it, we're all going to put some guilt on our kid – whether it be for leaving not a square of toilet paper in the bathroom or for not getting their math done for the day. And we're all going to beg them to complete a task eventually. (I start with "Would you please...?" go on to "Please do..." then "Do it *now*." But if it's still not done... I'm sort of stuck with yelling and screaming or begging. Or doing it myself, but that's not feasible if it's *their* math problems.)

We've all bribed our kids – even though most of us swore we'd never do it. It might not have been with candy in the check-out lane –

it might have been a promise of a story read together or a hug when those last few problems were done – but we've all resorted to a bribe eventually in return for *something* we wanted them to do.

In the end, all we can do is try to use Guilt and Begging *consciously* and *conscientiously*.

And, of course, carefully.

Done well – not too much, for things that are important, well-separated, being clear about issues and results, and when everyone is reasonably mentally stable with each other – Guilt and Begging make it clear that there is a problem and a solution. But even better, these tools make it clear that your kid has *agency* and the ability to improve this situation in the future.

And helping our children develop *agency* is a critical part of not just helping them grow up into adults but *allowing* them to do so. Because, in a lot of cases, the safety net we try to put out there to catch them if they fall is so close to the tightrope they are trying to balance on that their metaphorical toes can catch in it. Despite what one often hears in popular media, however, this isn't necessarily a huge problem for homeschoolers as compared to kids in school; homeschooling parents often know our kids so well that we feel comfortable giving them *more* freedom and agency than kids in school get with parents who may only see them for a few hours a day and simply aren't aware of how much they really can handle and just where that supportive hand needs to be. My personal experience has been that a lot more 'helicoptering' happens with school parents and kids than with homeschoolers.

Trust your own assessment of your kid's capabilities, let them go a little beyond what you think is possible... and sometimes nudge them to go a little farther than what *they* think is possible. Guilt and Begging is often a part of the 'negotiation' between parent and child as to where those limits are and how to push them. (Remember Vygotsky's Zone of Proximal Development in Chapter Four!)

One last warning about using Guilt and Begging. Make sure that there's a connection from what you are asking of your kid(s) and the well-being and development of the child and that you aren't leaning on them more than necessary. We all have different places to draw that line – when I was heavily pregnant, or when I've had my chronic fatigue-conditions acting up I've needed help to be able to create an environment in which my children can thrive. That has meant needing them to cook, do laundry and dishes, care for the animals, some light cleaning, caring for each other, and helping each other with schoolwork. I'm perennially in charge of things the kids would have legal or physical difficulty doing, such as scheduling, paying bills, driving places, shopping, and long-term planning, including for our family's education. A single parent who is homeschooling may have to lean harder on one or more of those areas than I've had to, and parents with only one child may not have to lean on any of that at all.

But there is a line between improving the child's environment and leaning on the kid for my own convenience. In teaching them to stand on their own I don't want to turn them into *my* crutches, after all!

My stick of butter example walks that line pretty tightly, and I'm aware of that. Asking them to get me a cup of water instead of getting up to get my own walks that line. But asking them to make me a cup of tea when I can barely see for sneezing doesn't. And asking for that cup of water when I'm half-dead from heat or exhausted with the chronic fatigue doesn't (even if my husband thinks it does).

Every family's line between holding the kids back and turning them into crutches will be different, of course... and there's no 'right' or 'wrong' about where any of us choose to draw that line. Nor when the line moves because of illness – or, hopefully, moves the other way because of recuperation.

In my birth-family things move back and forth. My dad is in his eighties and very spry, but he needs help with certain things and my sister (who lives three hours away instead of the thirteen hours that I do) ends up doing those things for or with him. (I tend to get given other 'assignments' – everything from looking up obscure research articles and interpreting them for him to knitting copper wire – since I'm too far away for regular interaction.) He's always been there to support us both from tutoring us through college math to listening when we needed to cry... to homeschooling us when school was a terrible fit. Sometimes he's leaning on her... and sometimes she's leaning on him. And just like a pyramid – or a ladder – they can both reach higher because they have each other. They argue and complain, but overall, they're both happy to have each other.

I've had friends with other chronic conditions who felt it was important not to lean on their kids at all – sometimes exhausting themselves in the process. I've had contact with a few people who seemed to go the other way on things, as well. But on the whole, my experience of homeschoolers is that we are more likely to give our kids agency and involve them in the vibrancy and reality of our lives in a healthy way than we are to either baby them or crush them with our expectations.

It seems like a fine balance, but in reality that 'line' is often a mile wide.

Trust yourself.

You'll be fine.

TO DO (or try) to Get CHORES done
(and give the kids some agency)

- *The Family Democracy – the most effective, at least for our large, argumentative family, but the hardest to believe.*
- *Cash handouts*
- *Chore charts with immediate gratification*
- *The Race*
- *The Leaderboard*
- *The Bean Counter*
- *Guilt and Begging*

Chapter Six

How to Teach Your Kids

WAIT A MINUTE. ISN'T THIS book supposed to be about how to cope with being a *homeschooling* parent? All of this so far has been about *other* stuff that could apply to pretty much *any* parent in *any* parenting situation.

Well, yes. That's true.

Homeschooling is parenting on overdrive

AND BY THAT I DON'T mean that we do everything for the kids or protect them from everything that might challenge them... or at least not more than parents with kids in school do. (Actually, as discussed at the end of the last chapter, the majority of us tend to do that a lot *less* than parents with kids in school... at least after the 'deschooling' period, which we'll talk about more below.)

What I *do* mean is that – while parenting is 24/7 for everyone who has a kid – there is a distinct difference between having them in school for six hours a day (or eight or ten, counting travel, aftercare, activities, sleepovers, etc.) and having them *with* you most of that 24/7. That difference can often be summarized as Quality Time compared to Quantity Time.

You need both, of course. Spending all your time together and hating it (zero Quality Time) would be as bad as spending zero time together and being perfectly happy – at least from the perspective of building a lasting relationship with your kid. Which brings up another point: *homeschooling is all about that relationship with your kid... and your co-parent (if you're lucky enough to have one)... and your other kids.* It's also about your relationships with friends and other family members, though unless you're living in a multi-generational or other combined living experience it's probably at a slight remove. The goal, if you want to think about it that way, is to be *The Brady Bunch* and not *Everybody Loves Raymond.* (There's a lot of love around *ELR*, but the amount of frustration... I think we could all do without that.)

We, as homeschooling parents, have the additional responsibility of (usually) being our child's primary instructor – or perhaps their 'educational coordinator', seeking out and obtaining resources and opportunities from a vast smorgasbord of possibilities. It's can be one of the greatest delights – and it can be incredibly intimidating, even to those of us who come at it with a lot of experience or education (or experience *in* education). Learning and teaching at home is a different beast than at school, and we-the-homeschooling-parents have to be willing to be flexible, to seek out support for ourselves and our children, and to be excited about learning new things alongside them (as well as re-learning things that we may not have really absorbed, or even appreciated, in our own go-round with the Educational System).

The goal is to give our children a better educational experience than they would have received in school. Exactly how to do that effectively is a challenge that changes with each child as they grow – and from child to child. It's not an 'insurmountable obstacle.' It's a set of exciting challenges that will make *us* grow and develop and become ourselves in ways we may never have imagined.

For example, while there are a rather significant number of public and private school teachers and administrators who choose to homeschool, there is also a rather significant number of homeschooling parents who choose to become school teachers once their own children are grown or have enrolled in school (after some years at home). Part of this is because these former homeschoolers are people who have a great deal of experience in helping children learn... but as someone who myself has no inclination to teach in school (although I enjoy teaching), I can tell you that is not enough. These are people who discovered a hitherto untapped facet of their selves during their time as a homeschooling parent. They are people who often left far more lucrative careers for 'a few years' to solve an otherwise insoluble problem for their kids... and ended up discovering that teaching can be rewarding or that they want to change the Education System and can best do that from the inside.

Additionally, there are people who discover whole new areas of interest for themselves – outside education – by following their kids' interests, which may manifest in their lives as new careers or new directions to established careers.

The learning part of homeschooling isn't an *end* for parents any more than it is for our kids. It's a process or a 'journey'... and that means we're going somewhere. The flexibility of a homeschooling lifestyle means that we have the opportunity to try different directions... sometimes tugging the rest of the family along with us, and sometimes being dragged along with them to the increase of all our mutual knowledge and our understanding of possibilities and potential.

Teaching and parenting are not two different things.

(No matter where your kids are educationally, emotionally, or otherwise.)

SOME KEY POINTS OF THE *Brady Bunch* for me are that (1) they have a third adult around to help manage all those kids; (2) the parents took care of themselves and each other *and* their relationship; and (3) they treated the needs of each of the kids individually, knowing that *fair* and *equal* are not the same thing. Of course Jim and Carol Brady didn't homeschool – but those lessons of good parenting also apply to good *teaching* for a homeschooler.

We all know that the kids learn more from what we model for them than we really appreciate. They learn from others, too, of course, but when we homeschool we are reducing the number of role models that they spend as much time with.

This is good and bad both. On the one hand, we are able to be choosier about what is modeled for them – we don't have to worry about that teacher who talks down to them and clearly hates her job (we all had one of those... hopefully just the one), what misinformation and disinformation they are picking up from other kids, or copying the bullies on the schoolbus. On the other hand, those swear words that shocked grandma? We all know they heard them from our mouths and no one else's. And we're losing the potential *positive* role-modeling from great teachers (we all had one of those, too... hopefully way more than one) who adored kids and teaching and everything to do with their lives.

The *good* news is that we are *still* not our kids' only role-models, though we may have to hunt a little for the others. The *better* news is that we can often make sure that *all* those other role-models are positive ones. Yes, our kids will have to learn to deal with difficult peers and superiors someday, but only in K-12 education are they unable to make a choice to leave if the situation is truly unbearable. Leave the grown-up sized problems for later and ease into them. Your kids will figure it out as they grow up, and they will be okay.

So... on to teaching.

Goals... again

YOU WON'T BE SURPRISED BY now to read that the first thing I'm going to tell you is to clarify your goals and those of your co-parent and your kids. If you are bound and determined for Suzy to make it into

NYU's Tisch School of Art and your co-parent wants Suzy to join the Peace Corps and *Suzy* has her eye set on a job in the finance industry... you might be working at cross-purposes. Similarly, you might not be seeing eye-to-eye if you'll be horribly hurt when Suzy says what you do looks too hard and she never wants to have kids and certainly won't homeschool them if she does (most kids say this at some point... I did, and look at me now with six). And if you expect Suzy to have a post-High School plan and she doesn't really care, that can be really scary for a parent – homeschooling or not (keep in mind that it's often those last two years of High School where the idea that a Plan can be useful kicks in for a lot of kids).

We often take it upon ourselves that it's somehow a reflection on us as people and parents if our kids don't want to be like us or have a Plan or disagree with our goals for them or choose a different religion (even if we agree with their personal morals) or choose a certain S.O. or... Homeschoolers or not, we take all this stuff upon ourselves that really isn't about us at all. As homeschoolers we're in the interesting situation of being *closer* to our kids so that we can see who they are as human beings who are as different from us as our best friend or our sibling... and also *closer* to our kids such that we feel they should 'get us' and accept our ideas a bit more.

Finding that balance is – as always – a matter of being explicit about what we believe so that we can make rational decisions. That includes rational decisions about teaching and helping our kids meet academic or other educational goals in order to reach *their* futures.

What we've always told out kids is that they need a Plan. They don't have to *stick* to the Plan – it's not written in stone – but they should have one so that while they're figuring out what they really want to do they're not just treading water or swimming in circles.

We've also told them that, if they *don't* have a Plan, they should work towards the *hardest* thing they can think of while they're figuring things out – because then whatever they change their minds to do will be easier and they won't have as much catching up to do.

Your Wise Parental Advice to your kids may vary from this. But talk to them about it, and keep talking about it more as they get older and need to hone in on a workable Plan.

And now for the details...

Homeschooling Styles

The first thing that's helpful is to decide what your homeschooling *style* is. But don't worry, it's not set in stone either!

Most of us start close to the upper left corner of the diagram, largely because that's all we know. Our only model for 'homeschooling' is what we saw in school – and we go with what we know.

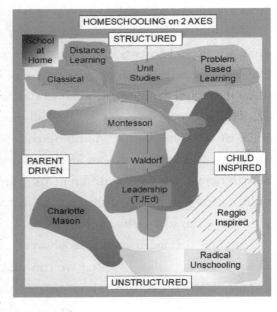

In this 'school at home' model the kids sit at desks – or a table; they have daily assignments that must be covered; the parent needs to teach all the material – or find some alternate method to present the material to the kids. The alternate method may be a video course, an in-person class, or something else that looks... a lot like school.

This is the most obvious approach... and it is also *hands-down* the *hardest* way to homeschool.

Why?

Because our homes are our homes and the kids have a different set of expectations for *home* and *school*. They aren't really going to object to *learning* at home, no matter how bad a fit school was for them – they've been learning things at home their whole lives, after all. But they are

146

almost certain to object to being *forced* to learn in the same way and to learn all the same things as they were being *forced* to learn in school.

The majority of families that I have met who gave up on homeschooling – not 'decided school was the better choice' after awhile, but *gave up* because homeschooling was too hard – were ones who *stayed* in this upper left corner of the chart. And by 'stayed' there I mean they stuck to their bought curriculum or online curriculum even when everyone in the family hated it and dreaded 'schooltime' and the following semester (or year) they felt that they'd 'given it a try' and homeschooling 'wasn't for them' because they couldn't see their way to trying something *other* than a bought curriculum. Perhaps not even a *different* bought curriculum. A few of them *did* switch the following semester or year – or, in some desperate cases, *month* – to a different bought curriculum... but they still didn't feel comfortable taking what worked, leaving the rest, picking up something else that worked better for one subject, or any of the other things that long-term homeschoolers end up doing.

Not all of us can really be that flexible or want to create our own schedules. And don't get me wrong: there *are* extremely successful homeschoolers who do manage to stick to those tight schedules and school-like atmosphere at home. But the folks who decide to stick with school-at-home really have to put a great deal of painful effort into corralling the kids, preparing lessons, grading, and more.

To put it in even starker terms, the NTI that most non-homeschooling families had to live with during Covid-19 was upper left corner on that chart. Everyone has experience with (or has heard about) all the problems with that approach by this point.

By contrast, there's the lower right corner – the 'radical unschoolers'. This is a school of thought that all you have to do is provide an interesting environment and the kids will learn all on their own.

Most of the homeschooling 'spectra' that I've seen run from the upper left to the lower right corner... which is why I put this one together myself. To me it's very clear that there are two different axes for the graph: Child-Inspired contrasting with Parent-Driven, and Structured contrasting with Unstructured. I prefer 'contrasting with' to 'versus' because most of us end up using a little bit of this and a little bit of that and don't sit firmly in any one spot (though there are some of us who do). I also like the idea of two axes, because that gives us an entire landscape of options and color to choose from.

> **DEFINITION**
> **NTI is short for 'Non-Traditional Instruction.' This is the catch-all term used by schools for their efforts to provide online education during the Covid-19 pandemic. It often included multi-hour Zoom calls and required logins. Not to be confused with online educational companies and curriculum providers that have historically focused on the homeschooling market.**

My family has wandered around the center right – we began with Waldorf because the mother of our neighbor family was a Waldorf teacher when our oldest ones were babies and I became enchanted with the arts-based Waldorf approach. Our family's natural inclination is towards Problem-Based Learning, and Unit Studies just make sense with a large family, but the TJ Ed/Leadership approach has also appealed a great deal to me. And we dip into Unschooling simply as a result of my energy levels. I started calling us "Waldorf-Inspired Secular Eclectic UnSchoolers – because WISEUS is better than a wiseass" before my oldest was ten.

So, what are all these things?

Let's take a look at them one by one:

- **School-at-home:** exactly what it sounds like and we discussed it above.
- **Distance Learning:** any type of online or correspondence-type education, including NTI. There are a number of companies that are well-known in the homeschooling community – such

NOTE!

I'm mentioning curricula I'm either familiar with or that people I know have tried... I am *not recommending* any particular curriculum. I do things *à la carte,* and strongly believe in fitting the learning materials to the child and parent.

So if you ask me what *you* should use, my answer will be that it depends. If your child has ADHD or is a neat nut or is very artistic you'll choose a different approach and materials than if your child likes to sit still or is a compulsive slob or hates to draw. Similarly, if you-the-parent (or your co-parent) absolutely go nuts if there is a mess left over from a project or needs a great deal of structure in your life to feel comfortable... you'll have a different set of needs than the parent who feels an empty table means they haven't done anything or that a busy schedule is stressful.

Sometimes we don't even know how strongly we feel about something until we try it and it doesn't work. Pick what you think will work for you... and be willing to switch it up when you find out it wasn't a good fit!

(And the best way to try things out is to buy the *smallest* unit of the curriculum you can to start: *one* workbook or *one* project or *one* subject. With that smaller investment in what you're trying it doesn't feel so financially painful if switching something out makes more sense for your family.)

as OakMeadow, Power Homeschool, and the Calvert School – that have figured out how to do entire curricula well. Newer entrants to the field keep cropping up, like GamEdAcademy which uses Minecraft to teach everything from History to Math. Unlike NTI, many of these other online and correspondence courses allow the student to self-pace and to log in at their own convenience. Courses that have a discussion component (such as many of the AP courses for High Schoolers at www. aphomeschoolers.com or the courses at Royal Fireworks Press) will require a specific login time and keeping up with the class, but those are usually chosen on an *á la carte* basis and the child and parent can make a choice about how many such rigid commitments the family wishes to support.

- **Classical:** this uses the approach of Latin Schools where there is a Grammar stage, a Logic stage, and a Rhetoric stage, roughly corresponding to Elementary, Middle, and High School. Memoria Press and Classical Conversations are two of the popular homeschool curriculum producers in this area and Susan Wise Bauer's book *The Well-Trained Mind* will set you up to do it yourself.

- **Unit Studies:** a topic is approached as a 'unit' and the various 'subjects' are incorporated through study of the 'unit'. For example, a unit on frogs might cover biology and ecology (raise frogs, dissect them, study the life-cycle), physics (Volta's famous discovery of 'bioelectricity'), literature (stories of frogs), history (has it ever really rained frogs?), home economics (cooking and eating frog legs), mathematics (exponential growth in the absence of predators) and so on. Unit Studies is often popular with multi-child families where units can be planned so that children at different ability levels can join in, but some of the most elaborate units that I've seen were created by one very enthusiastic mom for her son, an only child. Our library has a program where a teacher (including a homeschool teacher) can ask for a study-box to be assembled – they take the topic and the age-range and find all the coolest books and videos in the library system on that topic... they even check them out for me before I get to the library and have them in a box ready to go (or three boxes when my oldest asked for materials on crime and recidivism... it was just a handful of items when we asked for stuff on electric cars). This is only a starting point, of course, but it's a good starting point!

- **Problem-Based Learning (PBL):** (also called *Project*-Based Learning) the topics are approached as a series of projects. For example, the FIRST Lego League my family participates in is a perfect example – the kids are faced with a series of problems. They have to begin by defining the problems before they even start to solve them. Building a doghouse might be a PBL project, but so could starting a business, creating a garden – or a community garden – or fixing a car. There are also suppliers like HomeScienceTools who sell complete PBL kits...though my experience is that no such item really stands alone if you really love it... and if you're flailing the kids (and yourself) to complete the kit it didn't grab your interests enough.

- **Montessori:** there is a ton of literature to read on Montessori-style education, all the way up through High School. A large emphasis here is on the individual learning needs of the child, a very reality-based and hands-on based series of skills-building projects or stations (in school). Typically, the child has a great deal more say about their learning process than in 'traditional' school. Time4Learning calls itself a Montessori-based homeschool curriculum, but the parents I know actually using this use Montessori suppliers for things like Cuisinaire rods and then plan out their own programs.

- **Waldorf:** technically this is **'Rudolf Steiner'** education, named after the Austrian founder, just as Montessori was named after the Italian, Maria Montessori. There is very much of a community vibe here, rather than individualism, with more fantasy play than Montessori and even a certain amount of mysticism (though as a homeschooler you can pick and choose the components that make sense to you and your family). There is still a strong component of hands-on, real work, but one of the most unique features is that art and song are woven throughout the curriculum. Christopherus Press and A Little Garden Flower (now called Waldorf Essentials) are two resources I've used with this approach. OakMeadow is also popular but has migrated so far towards satisfying Common Core/California homeschooling rules that many people no longer consider it really 'Waldorf'.

- **Leadership or Thomas Jefferson Education (TJ Ed):** this is a newer approach pioneered by the deMilles (who are still giving workshops!). I found that this made a great deal of sense to me because it explained how my kids had actually *behaved*. So, I would call this a 'developmental approach'. Younger kids in this system have an almost 'Waldorf' or 'Montessori' experience that segues into more PBL as they reach those mid-range years. As they pass through puberty their passions begin to erupt and take over their lives and they build their own sense of focus and direction. (You need to buy the deMilles' own books or lectures to learn about this one.)

- **Charlotte Mason Education (CM):** Ms. Mason was a British contemporary of Steiner and Montessori – all three of them came from very different backgrounds and had very strong opinions on how children ought to be educated. In CM Education there is a strong emphasis on observing and learning from the natural world. SonLight and The Good and the Beautiful have both gotten good reviews from friends.

- **Reggio Inspired:** this has come from a teaching approach developed after WWII in the Italian village of Reggio Emilia.

The teacher is viewed as a co-learner, discovering the world with preschool age students in an enriched environment. To my knowledge this approach has not been expanded to older kids, but it segues nicely into some of the other approaches that do.

- **Unschooling:** this approach is a less-extreme version of unschooling and is probably where my family falls a great deal of the time. Families may insist on getting academic work done in certain specific areas (say Math or English or Music) but be flexible about when, or even how, that is accomplished. The kids have a great deal of autonomy but parents may nudge them gently to get them to try specific activities and subjects. Parents accept the kids' personal goals as valid and help the child develop realistic plans to meet the more detailed or explicit goals. Learning is usually done via the kids' interests. (Right now, we're helping our nine-year-old develop a plan for her planned 'career' of unicorn-finding – not hunting, since that sounds too violent to her. We trust this is a phase... but we're suggesting she consider becoming a travel guide and lead other people on unicorn-finding trips... which gives us the opportunity to get her to study geography, finance [budgeting those trips], biology, and more.)

- **Radical Unschooling:** as mentioned in Chapter Two, children are assumed to be entirely responsible for their own learning process, with adults providing guidance when *asked*. Un*schooling* is not un*parenting* – every unschooling family has house rules, though the kids may have more say in those rules or help to enforce them (which, honestly, all kids do – we just may sometimes call it 'tattling' or 'babysitting'). People who are famous for inspiring this approach include John Holt and Dr. Peter Grey.

VERY FEW FAMILIES ACTUALLY 'LIVE' entirely in one of these regions of this chart, or at least not for very long. Most of us tend to use a mix, picking up what makes sense for our family along the lines of the kids' interests – edging towards the Child-Inspired and Unstructured corner – and then becoming a little more Parent-Driven and Structured when it comes to topics like Mathematics.

For now, just get comfortable with the idea that there *are* these axes and that you might start in the upper left corner (where most people do) but that may not be where you stay. Sliding a little bit right and down gives your family more flexibility – but you don't have to go so far that you feel like it's become a runaway train.

Keep in mind that the more Parent-Driven and Structured a family is, the more *work* it is for the parent. On the other hand, learning is often more *effective* when the family is in a Child-Inspired phase, but the lack of structure can end up making everything less *efficient*. It takes kids who really love structure to support Structured and Child-Inspired at the same time – our Lego team lives out in that quadrant, but it ends up taking over our lives (as do most team sports) and it works because the kids have been doing it for so long that they don't need a great deal of adult input (except to stay on track). Parent-Driven and Unstructured is also rather fraught territory – essentially you are asking your kids to do what you tell them, but not giving them a lot of expectations as to what and when you'll be asking them to do things... and my brief foray into that direction convinced me that it requires more effort from *me* than I was willing to put in.

Finding a balance where the parents aren't overburdened but the kids are learning what they want *and* what they'll need to be successful in whatever direction they are going (or you are taking them) takes some time. It's okay to try something out and discover that you really need more (or less) structure in your lives... and then readjust.

As a general guide when figuring out what your homeschooling style is *right now:*

- younger kids need more structure around the basic daily habits of hygiene, eating, manners, and so on – but they can usually entertain themselves (play is the child's work, to quote Maria Montessori) without needing much adult input... for academics and chores they need you to do things *with* them, such as reading, writing, drawing, listening;
- older kids in that mid-range from eight to twelve or fourteen need *lots* of adult input around how to keep themselves occupied (though they'll find plenty to do on screens) but are probably pretty decent on self-structuring the daily habits,

> *"Play is the child's work."*
> Maria Montessori

including things like fixing their own breakfast and letting you sleep in a bit... for academics and chores, kids of this range can usually allocate time for *short* spans, such as a few hours at a time or for one phase of a project, but you need to check in and do some of it *with* them if you expect to see specific results in a specific timeframe;

- teens need a different *kind* of adult input – more along the lines of a sounding-board – and may need assistance with those new issues of interpersonal attractions and body odor (if mom or dad doesn't say anything, who will?) and with all those 'adulting' things like paying bills and meeting the expectations of other people to whom they have made commitments... and when it comes to academics and chores they will probably be as much on their own (late morning to late night) schedule as you let them, but they still need you to check in with them daily or multiple-times-daily. (Remember that brain development –

especially those 'executive functions' that are all about self-control and self-discipline – don't really finish developing until the mid-twenties... giving your teens that support while they're still legally children will likely save you some heartache later, when they're older and more reluctant to accept help or out of your reach.)

Do I need to buy a curriculum?

YES...AND NO.

If it's going to make you feel better, it might be worth it. But most "whole" or "boxed" curricula that cover the entire range of things you want your child to cover in a single year run to the tune of several hundred dollars per grade level. *Plus* supplies. And many families that spent a huge amount of time researching and choosing those curricula end up discovering that they only want to use certain components of it – such as the English or the Science – and that they prefer a different approach for Math or Music or Art.

Additionally, most "boxed" curricula try to make your life easier by laying out a schedule for you to follow. This schedule is usually someone's brainchild about what *should* work or what *could* work and has not actually been tested against what actual homeschooling families can accomplish in a given period of time. A homeschooling friend tells me that Susan Wise Bauer, author of *The Well-Trained Mind* (a popular homeschooling how-to for Classical education), reputedly admitted once that her publisher felt she should have schedules in her book, so she threw them together and stuck them in. Dr. Bauer is a university History Professor, homeschooled her own kids, and was herself homeschooled. You might, therefore, imagine that her schedules are carefully crafted and tested... or at least reasonable. But I've read her book and those schedules in it are... intimidating.

Following even the most flexible-seeming schedule – say one that only has you doing 'deskwork' with the kids three days a week – can end up being less of a help and more of a guilt-trip if you're not careful.

All that said, I have a very dear friend who successfully used the SonLight (CM-based Christian) curriculum for most of her twenty-plus years of homeschooling of three children. The trick was that she used it as a *basis* and a *guide*, but didn't stick religiously *(ahem)* to their schedules. She also looked elsewhere for Math and Science curricula in particular as her kids' different learning styles and needs – and their interests – became apparent. Her oldest son is a classical pianist and pursuing a Ph.D. In Entomology and her daughter is an artist; Charlotte Mason supported their interests very well indeed!

Curricula can be excellent, but only if you keep in mind that they are written on paper, not stone, and that once that paper is in your hands you can twist it into all sorts of creative shapes to make it work for your family. (I don't think there's an *actual* Origami homeschool curriculum... but now I want to create one!)

Where many/most families *do* end up purchasing curriculum is for Math. And this includes my math-fanatical family as well. Children – even in the same family – can need *extremely* different approaches in order to absorb mathematical concepts. Not to mention that the methods used need to be ones that make sense to the parent as well, so that they can help with the eventual confusions – or you need to find someone, perhaps an older homeschooled kid who has used a similar curriculum, who can do that untangling for your kid.

I personally do everything *à la carte* simply so that it's easier to switch out something that isn't working well... and because I'm sort of 'allergic' to being told what to do.

Eeep! Too many choices! How do I decide?

In the end it doesn't matter *what* you choose to use if you're willing to approach it with what the philosophers call 'beginner's mind'. Approach what you are doing with your kids with an attitude of curiosity, interest, and willingness to learn and you can't really go wrong.

That does *not* mean that you can't ditch a particular text or project or curriculum. I learned that one the hard way — I used a trusted source to select the textbooks for my second daughter's AP Human Geography course and one of them was... utterly terrible. Maybe, if I had known the subject better myself, I could have done something more interesting with it... but this book

> **DEFINITION**
> **Beginner's mind: an attitude of curiosity, interest, and willingness to learn.**

managed to take a really interesting topic that we were all excited about and turn it into... a problem staying awake while I *read it aloud* to the kids. I ended up doing 'dramatic readings' to try to keep us all awake. Needless to say, the exam didn't go very well at the end of the year. Knowing what I know now, I'd look for other resources — at the time I felt overwhelmed and sure that this highly recommended text couldn't be *that* bad (and somewhat fearing that anything else would be *worse*).

Sticking with that book did my kid a double disservice: she didn't love the time we spent studying and she didn't do well on the AP test at the end of the year.

Uh-oh, you just said that WORD. Tests.

YEAH, STANDARDIZED TESTS ARE STILL part of our world as homeschoolers.

In some places families have no choice: homeschoolers are required to sit for the same standardized tests as all the other school-kids. Find out what the rules are where you live and follow them carefully. If you need more flexibility, contact your local Unschooling groups or private schools that don't follow the standard methods, like a Waldorf School, and ask how they handle state testing requirements. Homeschooled kids can also get testing accommodations for learning disabilities and testing anxiety, just like kids in school, so explore all your options.

In other places you may have more – or even complete – choice regarding standardized exams.

I live in one such place, and I absolutely *loathed* standardized tests as a child. So why do my kids take them?

In a word: college.

While we will be happy if our kids find other paths that fill their souls and support their stomachs, college is the default option in our family. And that means demonstrating in some way that college admissions officers can understand that our kids *have*, in fact learned a bunch of stuff and it's not just their adoring mommy or daddy who says so. (My husband, The Professor, says that grade inflation is so rampant in high schools in the USA that he wouldn't trust the grades given by a high school he wasn't extremely familiar with either.)

There are several ways to get external evaluations of your child's abilities. These include recommendation letters from bosses and coaches and scout leaders and so on. They can take courses at the local college – and that's actually looking like a better option for my more test-averse kids, since the grade is dispersed with multiple deadlines instead of just one high-stakes exam at the end. And they can *also* take standardized tests. Any combination of these things that establish how competent and skilled your kids are is fine.

Do what works for you and your kids.

My children recommend that the *important* tests – whatever they are for your kid, but at least the PSAT and the ACT or SAT – not be the *first* standardized tests they take. My oldest daughter's first standardized test was AP Physics 1 (Algebra-Based) – she got a 4 out of 5, but it was very stressful and felt she could have gotten a 5 out of 5 if she'd been calmer. (Which she proved the truth of by doing that on later exams.) Learning skills and test-taking skills are *not* the same.

But what about teaching all those advanced courses? You might be able to do that, but I can't!

Well... actually I couldn't either, as my total mess-up with Human Geography proved. (Thank goodness neither of the children who were doing it really wanted to pursue that field beforehand... though now, four years later we've all recovered enough that they are mentioning it's a really interesting topic... if only we had other resources...)

Or at least I couldn't all on my own.

Let me confide *my* real fear.

I was concerned that my kids would have a terrible experience in the *early* years – preK through fourth grade, say – because I don't like that stuff. I hate glue and paste and glitter and itty bits of things everywhere. I had a pack of small children (we always had a baby and a toddler and I was usually pregnant) so I didn't have the energy to clean all that stuff up. And I didn't want to get stuck – with my hoarder's tendencies – trying to figure out afterwards what to do with all the *Things* they created.

On top of that I don't really like being around small kids – other than my own. Even my friends' kids. I was actually like this as a small kid myself – and my couple attempts at babysitting outside the family were a disaster (I was fine with my own sister, which is why I dared have kids of my own). My brief dream of being like my sweet mother-in-law and having the house where all the neighborhood kids congregated quickly evaporated when that became a reality and I realized I was utterly miserable.

I prefer kids when they are old enough to start arguing about *Ideas* instead of... all that other stuff.

I did do all the Waldorf-y stuff with them when they were young – baking bread, gardening, cooking, knitting, woodworking, felting – and got the kids to be part of all those things. But they still can't cut paper in a smooth, straight line to save their lives. And all of those beautiful, gentle, art and music things sort of evaporated as our family grew and my energy levels shrank. We introduced screens when the youngest was two and... the younger three have never really helped bake bread, let's just say. And they have no idea how to knit.

But somewhere in the middle there we started running these Lego teams – that involve Programming and Problem Solving and Engineering and Analysis and Presentation Skills. And, man, but I *shine* as a coach there! More than half of my team has usually had ADHD and/or dysgraphia and/or... you name it, but they've been winning very consistently at the State level.

I would much rather spend a couple hours hunting for a great textbook on economics for my seventeen-year-old than the same amount of time with glitter and glue.

We all have our strengths. And our weaknesses.

And it is much, much harder to actually find people who are willing to balance your weaknesses with their strengths and vice versa than most homeschooling books imply... but that *is* kind of the whole point of a homeschool co-op. It was actually much *easier* to find people would do all those glitter-and-glue things in the early years – up to about fourth or fifth grade – which worked out well for me. My co-op friends were much more willing to delve into glue and paint and... all that stuff.

And that mom or dad in *your* homeschool co-op who, like me, tries to vanish when the paint and glue come out? She or he might be thrilled to lead a small group discussion for your tweens or teens on Great Literature or classes in Algebra and PreCalculus... or Ancient History or Physics. Or Car Mechanics. If you were the parent who was good with glitter and glue, let this other parent pay it forward by sharing their interests with your older child.

The good news is that once you have a handle (by making those *lists* I keep talking about) of what everyone wants out of the homeschooling experience and what really floats all your boats – you can start seriously looking around for the help you need. Most of us are better at more things than we give ourselves credit for – and have more resources than we can really believe are out there. (This is a good time to make another few lists, starting with one that includes all the things that *you* are good at and enjoy sharing with others. If you can get a handful of other parents to do the same, there's a good chance you can cover most topics that you'd want your kid to cover.)

For the younger and mid-range kids, 4-H and Scouts (of various sorts, including Boy, Girl, and Earth Scouts among others) are extremely reasonably priced and give a child access to an entire range of learning opportunities. Public libraries often have educational programs or can connect you with older people or specialists in the community who would be interested in teaching your kid a bit – befriend your librarians!

Remember that *kids* can take *adult-education* courses in everything from Herbology to Astronomy to Cooking (I did all of those myself as a middle or high schooler). And not just 'adult-education' classes – many two- and four-year colleges are happy to 'dual-enroll' high school and even middle school students. My husband took a programming class at their local community college (his father was also a student in the class) when he was in eighth grade. My oldest daughters spent their last year of high school taking courses at the four-year university where their father teaches – we have a number of friends whose children are doing the same.

And, of course, there are books and all of the entire Internet (though all of these options need some triaging).

By late middle and high school you may be seeing some career (or at least post-graduation) Plans forming in your kid's mind that can tell you where to focus your energies on looking for more ways to help them reach their goals. If your kid is considering Nursing, look for college-courses in Biology or Human Anatomy. If English isn't a love and your kid is able to communicate reasonably well – write a letter to a congressman, follow a recipe, enjoy a novel, whatever meets your and your child's list of goals for English fluency and competency – then don't worry about whether they have a solid grasp on the parts of speech and can explain grammar. (Since my kids are college-bound, writing a decent essay was a goal – but they've done all those other things as well.)

Math for the kid who isn't going into a STEM field can be fulfilled as 'Consumer Math' or 'Personal Finance' instead of becoming (or staying) a daily battle. Have them plan the family's meals for a week – or a month – within a budget, or consider going over your family's finances together. Or by filling out taxes and FAFSA forms together. (FAFSA is the Free Application for Federal Student Aid – this is one of the most critical pieces of paperwork to fill out if your child will be attending college.)

Your three goals as a homeschooling parent covering the higher grades are:

- to meet whatever your State (or National) requirements are;
- to fulfill whatever the requirements are for whatever program your kid will go to next (or is likely to in the near future); and
- to enjoy the last few years of homeschooling together

How do we accomplish these things? A good part of it is to *use what they are already doing by choice* and *acknowledge all the different ways to reach a particular goal*. If your kid(s) will be going to college – or other programs such as the military or an apprenticeship – you'll need to create a transcript, which isn't nearly as scary as it sounds. A transcript is really just an ad showing your kid in the best, most honest light possible.

Sounds nice, but I want *details* and *examples*

Fair enough.

We had to get creative with English, for example, because my kids love to read and discuss books but several of them kind of hate to write (so much for that thing about falling apples and trees), and because most colleges want to see 'eight semesters' of English on the high school transcript. We attended Shakespeare-in-the-Park (and studied the history of the plays, but not the plays themselves, beforehand) and watched a few movie versions of some of those plays. I counted all the fantasy and science fiction books they read as a course in... Science Fiction and Fantasy and managed to get them to read a few more of my own favorites! Several of my kids email their Senators and Representatives regularly and participate in online discussions (often gently correcting other posters' science). Eventually – because my particular kids are all about competition – they decided to participate in the Optimist International annual essay contest. When I put all of those things together, that certainly adds up to four years of high school English... even if I had to get creative with titles for some of those 'courses.' And there was no fighting with me because it was all things they were doing on their own already.

One of my other 'tricks' is that we also *don't* only count things done in 'that' semester or year for a particular course. We spent two years on AP US Government & Politics because that's a huge interest for our whole family. We joined a get-out-the-vote phone bank and wrote to our senators and congressman. We attended local protests and visited Washington, D.C. We read our textbook on family car-rides, stopping every few minutes for debates and clarifications and interesting tangents. We had a great deal of *fun* with it, and the *whole family learned together.*

Is this 'fair'? Absolutely. The *point* of homeschooling is to be flexible and self-paced and give your kid a chance to really absorb and understand the material. My kids can talk intelligently about any of the topics I list on their transcript, no matter how non-traditionally they learned it, and demonstrate that they know what it was all about – even *years* later – because they cared about it. (In Educationese, we call this a 'mastery-based approach' and it's been increasingly in vogue with private and public schools the last decade or so.)

There are also online schools and homeschool curricula that many middle and high school aged kids use very successfully. Power

Homeschool, Penn Foster, Calvert, OakMeadow and many more offer options where the entire curriculum is available online. If you want to do a piecemeal

> **DEFINITION**
> **Mastery-based is Educationese for an approach that focuses on mastering concepts and skills rather than just 'covering' them. The emphasis is on *depth* over *breadth*, although there is usually still a fair amount of breadth.**

approach, options like aphomeschoolers.com, Art of Problem Solving, Royal Fireworks Press and many others offer classes *à la carte*.

As with *every* school and educational system, there are trade-offs. My older daughters have taught themselves to play violin and piano – and they sound decent, but they didn't have the opportunities to develop more skill that they might have had in school. My sons are very good archers, but there are very few archery competitions open to them through 4-H. Some sports, like football or pole-vaulting, which is a sport that a number of former gymnasts go on to and that opens up another world of scholarship opportunities, are completely unavailable outside of schools.

It's a choice, of course, and there are good reasons to choose either way. If you want to choose to homeschool through the upper grades there are lots of ways to do it. Don't let the complexity of the material your kid needs to cover scare you off!

So just where do I find all these amazing options and people to teach my kids?

You do have to hunt a bit – but often they jump out at you from homeschooling social media groups and sites.

Sometimes these are school-based programs where the rules were written such that homeschoolers can still participate... and it requires finding out that such things exist. If your children have particular interests and your Google searches are only turning up school-based programs, contact the organizers and ask if they accept homeschoolers – and if there is a local team they can join or whether you can start up your own. Some schools are very welcoming to homeschooler participation – and even if limited by state or district policy they may still be supportive and help you get started or make connections.

My four oldest have all participated in Model UN, Model State Government, and Model Federal Government programs through The Y – and the coach of their homeschool team is absolutely spectacular. I found out about the opportunity only because this wonderful lady – who also coaches teams for some of the larger (and more academically impressive) local public middle and high schools – happened to be homeschooling one of her kids the year my oldest daughter was in tenth grade. This highly experienced coach posted on social media that she was willing to run a team for the homeschool community. Her daughter was actually back in public school (at that impressive public high school) later that year, but five years later that coach was still running our homeschool team. Why? Because our team is so small – usually about eight kids compared to the fifty or hundred in her school-based teams – that she enjoyed having the opportunity to get to know the kids individually.

There are also community-based opportunities out there if you keep alert.

The kind, older lady who runs our local Optimist International Club – and the 4-H programs there, including archery – caught my attention to suggest enrolling my kids in a summer gardening program a few years ago. We found out about the archery programs initially simply by noticing a sign in front of the Optimist Club building, along the side of the road we drove up and down almost every day. (The Optimist Club also became the home for our Lego teams after I realized that the entire goal of this organization is to run cool activities for kids!)

Soccer and gymnastics I had to hunt out on my own, but there's a local parent who regularly recruits kids for middle school and high school competitive homeschool basketball teams. Another runs a tennis team, and a third has a homeschool track team. And others who post about art courses (some of which my most artistically enthusiastic daughter took).

Cottage school programs sometimes go up through the upper grades, and then there are those college courses as well.

In Kentucky, 'dual-enrolled' high schoolers (those attending high school but taking college courses) pay less than $100 per credit hour at public universities, as of approximately 2016 – which is something like a tenth or less compared to taking those courses if they later enroll as fulltime college students. However, all those 'dual-enrolled' college credits will let them graduate with a college degree faster. (Or, as in my oldest daughters' case, graduate in four years, but take much more advanced courses.) One homeschooling family that we know has their children starting college courses in about ninth grade at our local four-year university (where my husband teaches) and using that for their *entire* curriculum; their kids will collect a four-year college degree simultaneously with their homeschool high school diploma.

And since high schoolers from public and private schools enter with such a wide range of preparedness, even many four-year colleges offer lower-level courses that might be appropriate for younger kids. Things such as basic courses in English or Pre-Algebra. But the courses are aimed at adults, so the teachers usually don't 'talk down'. Additionally, the kids get to pick and choose (with your help and guidance and financing) courses that fill their souls as well as meet their requirements and may have access to courses that are rarely available in high schools. My second daughter took two semesters of Arabic at our local university, for example, filling her 'foreign language' requirement for the colleges she wanted to apply to after high school.

Another wonderful option is the Great Courses series of video courses – many of which are available for free at public libraries and others available by DVD from the company (or even videotapes on eBay). Again, the courses are *aimed* at adults, but my six- and eight-year-olds found that they enjoyed learning about fractions from the course on basic math.

Other free online courses and helpful sites include Khan Academy for all sorts of (mostly?) STEM topics, DuoLingo for languages, and MIT's OpenCourseware free college courses taught by actual MIT professors. And that doesn't even touch on the vast array of not-free options!

Does your kid love cars like mine does? See if he'll hangout at a mechanics' shop and make friends – or a go-kart track or even a demolition Derby. Or just a simple car show where people have brought their cars to show off and are just *so excited* to talk to you about cars. (My car-crazy son and I hit a different, smaller show a few months ago and spent close to an hour talking to a lady about her exotic Honda Beat and the other cars she and her husband and *her* eighteen-year-old son fix up for fun. We got her number, but my sixteen-year-old son – who regularly emails our senators and argues with people on car websites – has so far been too shy to give her a call... but there she is!)

There are Guilds for Weavers and Embroiderers and Quilters and Woodworkers and other crafters – and most of those people are thrilled to share what they love with younger people... or know someone who is. It's often easy to find model-train hobbyists – who might include retired railroad engineers – or flight-training for kids with retired pilots. The Co-operative Extension (there's one in every US state, they run 4-H) has Master Gardener programs. When my child who wanted to be an entomologist and I kept bees for a few years we found ourselves invited to the local beekeeping organization's meetings.

Sometimes it's just about keeping your eyes open and digging a little... and then not being too shy to take up on opportunities that are offered. Honestly, being shy and not wanting to admit I don't know something have been my biggest hurdles — and letting my kids see how I struggle with that and work to overcome it have been great life-lessons for them... and for me.

If you want to keep homeschooling all the way till you hand them that diploma... you can do that! The key, always, is that it has to be something that you and your kid want and that your family can support. Know your goals, decide what counts as a 'win' and you can make it happen!

TO DO in order to actually TEACH your kids

- *decide where you are – for right now – on the axes. Are you more Parent-Driven or Child-Inspired? Are you more Structured or Unstructured?*

- *how much do you want to push away from where your current comfort point is?*

- *Buy what curriculum you need...*

- *but don't get emotionally attached to following the schedules too closely*

- *and don't be afraid to ditch something that isn't working. Your time and your kids' time is too valuable to waste on poor quality materials. (And you can always try reselling it on eBay, Craigslist, or at your local homeschool resale shop!)*

- *Look for opportunities for your kids to learn from or with other people*

- *other people often advertise on social media activities that they are running or involved with... or even repost what they have heard about*

- *car shows, crafters' guilds, and other places where people interested in what your kid needs or wants to learn are gathered are helpful*

- *Establish what your kid knows using standardized tests, college courses, or recommendation letters from adult mentors*

- *Use what's free – but don't ignore options that cost (sometimes you really do get what you pay for)*

- *Take longer to do a 'course' of study than a school might – if you can have fun with it!*

- *The actual details are less important than approaching learning with 'beginner's mind' and ENJOYING THE JOURNEY!!!*

Conclusion

Why Neil Gaiman is Right About Everything (including homeschooling)

IN THE END, THE IMPORTANT decision isn't whether you use a particular curriculum or follow a certain approach for chores or academics or even whether you homeschool or use one of the many, many other options out there to meet their academic and social needs.

The important decision is whether you are taking the time to enjoy being with your kids and giving them the time to enjoy being with you and getting to know you as a person.

No matter what's going on in life, Enjoy Your Kids.

> **No matter what's going on in life,**
>
> **Enjoy Your Kids.**

They're *your* kids. They came from you (one way or another) and they're going to be special, unique human beings because they're yours.

Don't get caught up in all the crazy things they are doing, or whether they are going to make it to the Olympics (as spectators? as competitors?) or Congress or Carnegie Hall or MIT or whether they ate their broccoli today or whether they know as much math as their cousin or the next-door neighbor kid or whether their handwriting looks truly, unbelievably illegible (that's what computers and word-processors are for). But don't underestimate them either – because maybe they *will* go to the Olympics or Congress or Carnegie Hall or MIT. Give them your best – including your faith in them as human beings and as lifelong learners – and let them be themselves.

Don't get hung up on whether you have the *right* curriculum or have them in the *right* activities or are making sure they do *enough* chores (or that they *never* have to do chores). Homeschooling is just parenting. You've got this.

And don't let the fear of making mistakes while homeschooling your kids (or public-schooling them or private-schooling them or after-schooling them or unschooling them) let you not try whatever it is that makes sense to you-the-parent (and your co-parent and the kid in question and...). There will be things you do 'right' and things you do 'wrong' and chances are you won't actually be sure which is which for twenty or thirty years.

Remember: we only make mistakes when we are trying to do something differently. It means we are doing something. And doing something to help your kids and your family is the critical step.

The important thing is to take care of yourself and those you love. Don't change your mind about homeschooling on the days that are hard.

I tell people that I decide to homeschool every day. Sometimes multiple times a day. (Sometimes multiple times an hour.) There will always be days when things go completely sideways. When you had to

> **We only make mistakes when we are trying to do something differently**

actually *sit* on your *kid* to get enough liquid Benadryl into him to control his allergy-induced temper tantrum. When your kid gets forgotten at the big gymnastics show and you have to stand there watching her crying. When Child Protective Services or the School District shows up because your nosy neighbor reported you instead of coming over and asking some polite questions. When your three-year-old throws himself over the new balance beam and cuts his head open and needs stitches at nine p.m. on a Sunday night.

When you have a headache and that's the day the kids have to end up in an argument every five minutes. All. Day. Long.

When the school that is down the road seems oh-so-attractive. It's even *free*, remember?

But in a day... or maybe a little longer... some of those things will change or go away.

Your violently allergic (or should that be allergically violent) child is now the most mature and trustworthy young person you've ever met.

Your little girl declares that not only is she not quitting gymnastics, but *next* year she'll be on the *team* so that she'll never be forgotten again.

The Child Protective Services social worker (or School District official) tells you that it was actually nice to come to your house and see someone doing such a great job.

Your three-year-old amazes the doctors by telling them "thank you" after begging them to stop the whole time they were sewing him up.

Your kids who sounded like they were practicing for the WWE version of the Presidential Debates are cuddled up together on the sofa recording Christmas carols – in July, for some reason.

This is more than a 'these days too shall pass' reminder.

You need to take care of yourself. You need to let other people take care of you when they will – and ask them to if they don't volunteer. (And not take the 'no' answers personally. People have their own things. It's not about us, usually.)

It's good for the kids if you take care of yourself. It's also good for them if they get to take care of you a bit, too. It's good for them to learn to respect you as a human as well as a parent.

But really, you have to take care of yourself because
being a homeschooling parent is

REALLY PRETTY AWESOME

and you should enjoy this time.

Being a homeschooling parent is
REALLY
PRETTY
AWESOME
and you should enjoy this time.

You might be a homeschooler if...

... your kid/s spend most of their learning hours at home

... your kid/s spend a lot of time online

... your kids spend a lot of time outside

... you spend a lot of time looking for learning resources

... your kid/s spend a lot of time pursuing their interests

... you spend time learning things you are interested in

... you share your interests with your kid/s

... your kid/s share their interests with you

... your kids spend a lot of time creating/building

... your kids spend a lot of time reading

You may be using whole purchased curriculum, pieces of curriculum, online curriculum, STATE provided curriculum, making up your own, or just following your kids' interests.

You may be doing this for a week, a month, a semester, a year, or all the way to graduation.

You may be doing it by choice, out of desperation, or because of external circumstances... while at-home, work-(for-pay)-at-home, work-away-from-home part-time, work-away-from-home full-time, single parent, two parent, multi-adult family...

Acknowledgements

No book is an island (or a rock), even if it is self-published.

To list out all the people who have taught me to be a mom - and a homeschooling mom in particular - would be impossible. People who have been especially critical in this progression (some of whom suffered through a rather awful first draft of this book or found a few particularly egregious errors) include: Jenny Griebenow, Daisy Pelletier, Jennifer Nelson, Pam Boughton, Sara Melton, Sara Mauch, Jenni McKim, Shannon Hughes, Angie Mobley, Erika Markert, Kerri Schleiffer, Jes Francis, Jennifer Pearson, Patty Reuther, Renata DeWees, Marsha Howard, Erin Krumhansl, Kelly Hill, David Aronoff, Jalene Hornbuckle, Cindy Bagley, Jackie Hawkins, Cameron Howard, Eboni Cochran, Jonah Safar, Stephen Young,... and so many others. There's simply no way to list everyone... Life is learning is homeschooling is life...

I am grateful to my parents for homeschooling me and for giving me the encouragement and opportunity to write. Thanks particularly, Baba, for letting me continue to homeschool through high school so that I could keep writing. You were so right that I might not have time later... but wrong that I might not have inspiration!

And thank you also to my sister, Hamsa, who was my first student, my good friend, and who always, always, always has my back when it counts.

I'm grateful to my 'long-suffering' husband, Shamus. Twenty-five years, six kids, and counting (years, not kids!). He has supported me in all my crazy endeavors, through some pretty deep depressions, the loss of my mom, and all the crazy that comes with having six kids (which was his idea, btw). I couldn't ask for a better best friend... though he needs a little work as a proofreader. (Not his fault, usually I do that for him and his grad students.)

And no statement of gratitude for my husband would be complete without mentioning his awesome parents and family... who are also supportive of homeschooling and other insanities.

When we instituted our Family Democracy in January 2020, the kids decided to also institute a daily hour of Quiet Time to let me write. That sort of turned into me writing all day long and them coming to get me for all those little things like preparing food, solving disputes, driving them places, and, oh yeah, homeschooling. They have been remarkably supportive and encouraging and do an amazing job supporting each other so I can write as well. The sheer number of meals they have prepared (often embarrassingly late when I forgot), the driving they have done (sometimes letting me type, other times reading aloud to everyone while the older kids drove - kids with permits and licenses rock!), the times they have checked the younger kids' math or taken each other outside so I could have quiet... Thanks guys.

My oldest child, Meenakshi, took time out from her summer research to read through a draft of this book in detail and gave me the most comprehensive review. The remaining errors and insanity are mine, but she improved this book beyond all reason. Priyadevi and Griffin (kid #2 and kid #3) also read through that awful draft and had cogent, important comments.

The kids are now insisting I write the next homeschooling book, about how we teach math all wrong in our society. The title, that I have been threatening to use for years, is one of those mis-heard things said in the car: "Two Plus Three Equals Zebrapants". If the kids are willing to sacrifice my time with them to get these books written, I hope you'll be interested in checking on my progress with them at https://www.RisingDragonBooks.com

INDEX

Note from the author:

    It drives me crazy when I can remember a phrase or an idea from a book, but not locate it in the index - or I recall the first name isntead of the last name of an author whose work was referred to and it sounded cool.

    I've tried to include everything you might want to look up... but I'm sure I've failed. If you note things I got wrong or things I shoudl add, please contact me by email through at my website https://www.RisingDragonBooks.com

    If you are the first person to report an error or ask for a particualr update to the index, I'll let you know to send me a SASE to receive a FREE GIFT!

Keep an eye out for Kerridwen Mangala McNamara's
NEXT homeschooling book:

The Homeschooling Parent teaches MATH!
(Bringing Math to the Math-Averse, Parents and Kids Both!)

Available at fine online book retailers everywhere
in October 2023

About the Author

KERRIDWEN MANGALA MCNAMARA IS AN Indian-American with a Masters degree in Bacterial Genetics who lives in Flyover Country (the far northern end of the US South) with her husband, The Professor, four of her six children, three goats and a very old Great Pyr-Coonhound mix dog. The goats eat, the dog sleeps, The Professor plays chess, and the children largely unschool while Mangala writes. (The remaining children are in college – you can blame the oldest for the excessive amounts of math showing up in Mangala's fantasy novels... and the second one for better attention to staging of scenes.) Mangala is a former professional bellydance instructor, currently coaches FIRST Lego League teams, runs homeschool parent support groups, and used to enjoy knitting, crotchet and embroidering Temari balls but now is much more boring as she rarely does anything but write, argue economic theory with her 17 and 14 year olds, and wonder loudly if her 11 and 9 year olds do anything other than watch Minecraft videos. She owes her love of books and reading to her mother, who was a professional folklorist and could recite – from memory – stories from every nation in the United Nations.

(The picture was taken at one of her favorite local bookstores: The Rosewater in Louisville, KY.)

Learn about Mangala's upcoming projects (fiction and nonfiction both) and sign up for email updates at
https://www.RisingDragonBooks.com

Made in the USA
Las Vegas, NV
25 November 2023

81447870R10115